SUCCEED IN

Personnel Management

STUDENT BOOK

N5

Johan van Staden

OXFORD
UNIVERSITY PRESS
SOUTH AFRICA

OXFORD
UNIVERSITY PRESS

Oxford University Press is a department of the University of Oxford.
It furthers the University's objective of excellence in research, scholarship,
and education by publishing worldwide. Oxford is a registered trade mark of
Oxford University Press in the UK and in certain other countries.

Published in South Africa by
Oxford University Press Southern Africa (Pty) Limited

Vasco Boulevard, Goodwood, N1 City, Cape Town, South Africa, 7460
P O Box 12119, N1 City, Cape Town, South Africa, 7463

Oxford Succeed in Personnel Management N5 Student Book

ISBN 978 0 19 904134 3

First impression 2018

Acknowledgements
Publisher: Yolandi Farham
Project manager: Sarah Middleton
Editor: Sarah Middleton
Proofreader: Kim Van Besouw
Indexer: Sanet le Roux
Illustrators: Jane Commin, Warren Brink
Designer: Jade Benjamin
Cover designer: Cindy Armstrong
Typesetter: Aptara Inc.
Printed and bound by Castle Graphics Direct, Cape Town

The authors and publisher gratefully acknowledge permission to reproduce copyright material in this
book. Every effort has been made to trace copyright holders, but if any copyright infringements have
been made, the publisher would be grateful for information that would enable any omissions or
errors to be corrected in subsequent impressions.

Links to third party websites are provided by Oxford in good faith and for information only.
Oxford disclaims any responsibility for the materials contained in any third party website
referenced in this work.

CONTENTS

MODULE 4

QUALITY OF WORK LIFE

HOW TO USE THIS BOOK

Welcome to the Oxford Succeed series for TVET Colleges. *Succeed in Personnel Management N5* provides you with everything you need to excel. This page will help you to understand how the book works.

Flow diagram maps what you will learn in each module.

Learning objectives reflect the latest syllabus.

Headings direct you and tie in explicitly with the syllabus.

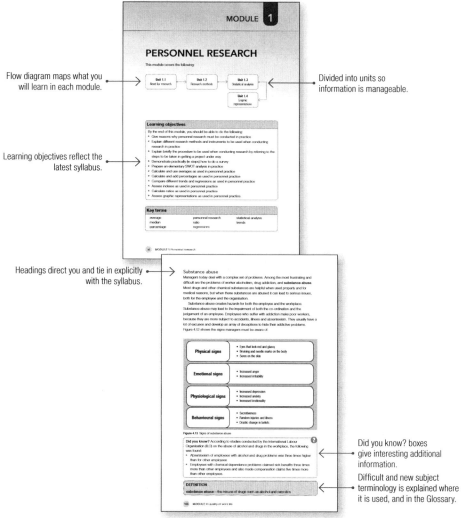

Divided into units so information is manageable.

Did you know? boxes give interesting additional information.

Difficult and new subject terminology is explained where it is used, and in the Glossary.

Other features:

Power break activities allow for discussion and revision.

Examples illustrate a point or provide practical worked examples.

Relevant Case studies and articles bring information to life.

Key points highlight core information, useful when studying.

- Diagrams, illustrations and photos provide information visually.
- At the end of every module, concise responses to the learning objectives are provided as a summary to use when studying.
- An Assessment section provides test and exam practice.

PERSONNEL RESEARCH

This module covers the following:

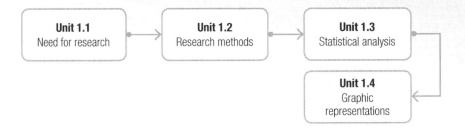

Unit 1.1	**Unit 1.2**	**Unit 1.3**
Need for research	Research methods	Statistical analysis

Unit 1.4
Graphic
representations

Learning objectives

By the end of this module, you should be able to do the following:
- Give reasons why personnel research must be conducted in practice
- Explain different research methods and instruments to be used when conducting research in practice
- Explain briefly the procedure to be used when conducting research by referring to the steps to be taken in getting a project under way
- Demonstrate practically (in steps) how to do a survey
- Prepare an elementary SWOT analysis in practice
- Calculate and use averages as used in personnel practice
- Calculate and add percentages as used in personnel practice
- Compare different trends and regressions as used in personnel practice
- Assess indexes as used in personnel practice
- Calculate ratios as used in personnel practice
- Assess graphic representations as used in personnel practice.

Key terms

average	personnel research	statistical analysis
median	ratio	trends
percentage	regressions	

Starting point

Julian Zipho has been the human resources manager at his company for the past five years. His company specialises in motor vehicle tracking systems. Julian's manager schedules a meeting with Julian to discuss personnel matters in general, but in particular she wants to discuss how the future and new developments in the industry will influence them. Julian's manager wants to be ready for what the future may hold for the employees.

For this reason, she asks Julian to conduct personnel research at their company. Julian needs to find out what their staff retention rate is, how long employees stay with the company and what the employees like or dislike about working at the company. He must also look at the latest trends and how those will influence them. For example, do they have enough personnel? Do they need to recruit new employees? Do they need to train the current personnel?

Figure 1.1 Julian discusses personnel research with his manager.

UNIT 1.1 **Need for research**

In Personnel Management N4 you studied basic management functions, enterprise functions and the organisation itself. In Personnel Management N5 we will study personnel research, how to recruit employees and how to maintain your human resources.

In today's competitive environment it is of the utmost importance to have the best human resources. This means that you should have the best skills, talent and competencies available to give your organisation the competitive edge for long term survival.

Part of human resource management is finding and maintaining the personnel that would help you reach your objective. Human resources are there to meet the day-to-day requirements as well as the future goals of the organisation. To be able to make the best possible decisions, you need to do **personnel research**.

> **Key point**: Personnel research is a systematic investigation of information to find a solution to a problem that involves employees in an organisation or institution.

From a human resources department manager's perspective, you will do research about the following areas or categories:
- Recruitment of employees (Module 2)
- Training and development (Module 4)
- Compensation/rewards for employees (Module 3)
- Maintaining employee relations (Module 4)
- Separation (Module 3).

Table 1.1 The categories and sub-categories of research

Recruitment of employees		
Recruitment policy	Factors influencing recruitment	Different strategies to assess candidates
Selection interview techniques	How to achieve employment equity	Selection of placement methods
Training and development		
Determining training needs	Factors influencing job satisfaction	The influence of job enrichment
The influence of job rotation		Career development opportunities in South Africa
Compensation/rewards for employees		
Performance evaluation problems that may occur	Different achievement evaluation techniques	How to compile a compensation package
Job evaluation systems	Different kinds of incentives	Problems when terminating an employee's service

> **DEFINITION**
>
> **personnel research** – the systematic gathering of information and facts to find a solution to a personnel problem

Maintaining employee relations		
Health and safety	Factors that influence labour turnover and absence	Methods of countering turnover and absence
The impact of technological developments	The influences of industrial actions	Communication between employers and employees
Separation		
Labour turnover rate	Counselling for retirement and retrenchment	Dealing with disciplinary matters

What are the reasons for personnel research?

Research will provide information on not only how to recruit the best candidates to fill vacancies, but how to keep them. Effective research will also make sure the organisation can stand up to its competitors. Personnel research informs organisations on how to adapt to the ever-changing demands of the internal and external environment. Research helps management to evaluate how the organisation's personnel are managed. Are the policies and procedures still valid and applicable or do they need to make changes?

Read the following extract from an article about engaging employees to see how research informs an organisation how to adapt to the ever-changing demands of the internal and external environment.

Employee engagement trends 2018

6 March 2018

Engaging employees to create effective teams that win in the workplace as well as in the marketplace is a common challenge across industries.

"Business plans don't deliver results, people do," says Alan Hilburg, president of advisory firm HilburgMalan.

Top five points:
- A central challenge facing human resource teams in the year ahead is the need to establish yourself as an integral business partner by being fluent in the language of business.
- Human resource (HR) teams must concentrate their energies on leadership and people in the organisation, rather than on administrative tasks.
- Human resources needs to be able to talk strategy to anyone in the business.
- Decisions are the key link between a company's culture and values: Your culture defines your decisions, which are guided by values.
- The millennial generation, which is entering the formal workforce in ever-greater numbers, want transparency and to be a part of something bigger than themselves.

Figure 1.2 Categories in human resource research

Read the two examples below to gain an understanding of what research entails. The first example describes a formal research article about technology and human resources, while the second example explains the purpose and objectives of Stats SA.

Example 1

The following is an abstract of the research article *Impact of Technology Advancement on Human Resource Performance* by Kamal and Ashish Kumar (2013).

> "According to Valverde et al. (2006), HR function is 'all managerial action carried out at any level regarding the organization of work and the entry, development and exit of people in the organization so that their competencies are used at their best in order to achieve corporate objectives.' It includes the actors as well as their relevant responsibilities and tasks.
>
> HR managers are facing many challenges in present business scenarios, like ... technological advances and changes in the political and legal environment. All these challenges increase the pressure on HR managers to attract, retain and nurture talented employees."

Example 2

Statistics South Africa (also known as Stats SA) is a national service in South Africa that provides official, accurate and useful statistics or information. The purpose of their research is to help the economy grow, and to improve general development and democracy in South Africa by using existing research and applying it.

Any organisation can order useful information (for example, monthly earnings in South Africa or the latest trends in the labour market) for their own benefit, free of charge.

UNIT 1.2 Research methods

Types of research

There are two types of research: basic (exploratory) and applied (operational) research.

Basic (exploratory) research is when you explore and find new information for the first time. This type of research is general and not for a specific organisation.

Applied (operational) research is when you apply research knowledge already obtained for your specific organisation or problem. You make the knowledge operational or practical to find a solution to your problem.

Research methods

There are many different methods an organisation can apply to do successful research, and there are many research methods available. Take note when you answer this question in the examination that although we discuss SWOT analysis separately, it can also be given as an answer for a research method.

We will be looking at the methods that mostly apply to you examinations.

Figure 1.3 Research methods

Historical studies

Historical studies investigate past information, such as events, data and documents, in order to use that information today.

As a research method you can learn from studying the past. You use the information that you gathered and apply it to your current situation or problem.

For example, your college is asked by the DHET to send in their attendance registers for the last five years. With this historical information, the DHET can research the attendance percentages of the students. They can determine what the trends of the students are, times when students are absent the most or whether there is a relationship between student absenteeism and students' final marks.

Case studies

This is a written or verbal explanation of a real-life event or situation. What you learn from a case study can help you to solve a problem, or it can be put into practice in your own situation.

For example, your lecturer gives you a newspaper article to read and then asks you to answer certain questions about the case. This helps you to learn from a real-life situation.

Did you know? Lecturers will use case studies to make your theoretical knowledge more practical by describing an event or scenario and then asking you questions.

Role play

With role play you are usually in a group, and each person acts out a particular situation. Each participant takes a specific role. This technique can be used in training or for research purposes where you learn from the role play. You can either be taught how to act (or not to act) in a situation or the role play can help with problem-solving. In the case of problem-solving, a group acts out a situation and then you or the group can find solutions on how to solve the problem.

Simulation

Simulation is the imitation of a real-life process or system. Simulation develops specific characteristics, behaviours and functions for a particular system or situation.

For example, trainee pilots do not immediately fly an airplane. They are first put into a simulator that is similar to an airplane's cockpit. There they can be put in different situations and learn to handle scenarios before they fly a real airplane.

Did you know? Role play and simulation are very similar, but role play will focus on a situation and simulation will focus more on a process or system.

Field study

This is where you try to find out what is going on in the world outside your organisation. During a field study, you would collect information outside your organisation or workplace.

For example, the most well-known field studies are surveys and observations. We will discuss these later in this module. Other examples are interviews and discussions.

Experiments

Experiments can be done in many different settings. Most people are familiar with scientific experiments that happen in a laboratory. A laboratory experiment is conducted in a controlled environment. Here you compare the dependent variable (control group) with the independent variable (experimental group).

The control group is known to you. The conditions stay the same, but the experimental group is unknown. You want to see the results and then compare these with what you already know.

Figure 1.4 Experiments can take place both in and out of a laboratory.

For example, you can compare students' examination results. The control group uses traditional paper textbooks. The experimental group uses a textbook in digital format on a tablet. Tablets are modern and still something new for education and training. In the end you can determine which group's results were the best.

An example from a human resources department would be that the human resources manager can use this method to do research about employees' absenteeism and productivity. The control group are those who work at set times, from 8:00 to 16:30. The experimental group are those employees who work flexitime. The human resources department can compare the groups and determine which group got the best results in terms of low absenteeism and high productivity.

Aggregate quantitative reviews

In order to understand quantitative reviews you will need to understand the difference between quantitative and qualitative research.

Quantitative and qualitative research

Let us start by explaining the difference between the terms quantitative and qualitative. These are two different but well-known approaches to research.

Quantitative research is numerical or statistical data (information), and includes data such as statistics and percentages. A quantitative approach answers questions about the relationship between these numbers, statistics and percentages.

Quantitative researchers use standardised procedures to collect data. Once the data is collected, researchers can draw conclusions. With numerical data, researchers can move from information that is general to specific and then confirm or disconfirm the hypotheses that were tested. They can also describe trends or explain the relationships between variables.

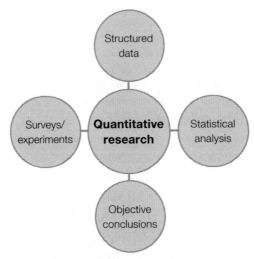

Figure 1.5 Different types of quantitative research

Qualitative research starts with general questions rather than specific ones. Researchers collect data through examination documents, observing behaviour and interviewing participants. Qualitative research is more all-inclusive and flexible. The findings are usually more tentative and form the basis of future studies.

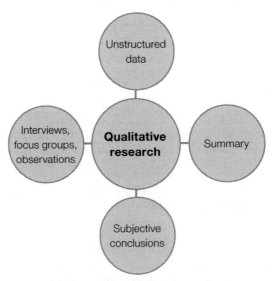

Figure 1.6 Different types of qualitative research

Quantitative research therefore is a study into social or human problems based on testing a theory, measured with numbers (objective), whereby qualitative research aims mainly to understand social life and the meaning that people attach to everyday life (subjective).

How to conduct a research project

It is very important to remember that the basic purpose of research is to seek answers to specific problems. Research projects take time, effort and planning.

Follow the process step-by-step. Steps help with the consistency of a project. When you focus on one step at a time, it will help you to conduct thoughtful and informative research.

Step 1: Define research problem.
Ask the question: What is the problem we, as an organisation, struggle with? Describe the problem in detail so there is no uncertainty about the research.

Step 2: Describe the objective(s) for the research.
Write down a brief summary of the problem. Explain it in terms that are familiar to all role players. By doing this everyone participating in the project will understand the problem and know what the goal is.

Step 3: Decide on the research method.
As discussed in the previous section there are different research methods available. You have to select the best method for your situation and one that will give you all the answers to your question or problem.

Step 4: Collect the information.
The information will depend on the research method you selected in step 3. The information will come from time-sheets, observations, interviews, online sources or previous studies. Be aware that the reliability of online sources varies greatly, so make sure the website you search is valid and reliable.

Step 5: Analyse and process the data.
This is the collection of facts and statistics. Data is the raw and unorganised information.

Step 6: Interpret the data.
You will explain the information so that everyone involved in the project can understand it.

Step 7: Compile a report.
In Steps 1–6 you gathered materials and information from several sources. In this step you put together or compose a report. This should give the reasons for the research, the process followed and all other relevant results obtained.

Step 8: Propose possible ways to solve the problem.

Figure 1.7 Defining a research problem is the first step in conducting a research report.

Surveys

All of us have been part of a survey at some point in time. Surveys can be found anywhere; in restaurants, at the petrol station or even at your college.

A survey is a detailed study of a specific topic, conducted by gathering data on people's attitudes, impressions, opinions, satisfaction levels, and so on.

At a restaurant or petrol station you might be asked to complete a survey to see your level of satisfaction with the services provided, or at your college, the campus management will ask your opinion on areas where they can improve by doing a survey.

For a survey to be a credible source or method of research, it must be conducted in such a way that it is accurate, valid and reliable.

Table 1.2 Three factors that make a survey credible

Accuracy	This means doing something correctly or precisely, without making mistakes.
Validity	This means the survey measures what it claims to measure.
Reliability	This means it is trustworthy. The survey should produce similar results if it were to be repeated.

Figure 1.8 Surveys can be electronic—they can be completed with a pen and paper or they might just be verbal.

Steps in conducting a survey

The following steps are useful for you to follow when you conduct a survey.

Step 1: Formulate the survey.
Keep in mind your overall goal or objective for the survey.

Step 2: Determine the procedures you want to follow.
Develop a questionnaire (this is also called the survey instrument).

Step 3: Describe the plan for the survey.
Do this by writing down the procedure you will follow.

Step 4: Analyse each question.
What questions do we want to have answered? Each question should be applicable to the overall plan of the specific research.

Step 5: Decide on the specific order of the questions.
The order should make sense and be easy to follow for a participant.

Step 6: Determine the standard for the survey.
With a standard you create consistency. The quality of each survey will also be the same if you have a standard.

Step 7: Give clear instructions on how to complete the survey.
To determine the standard, you must decide on the specific mode of collecting the data that will be used.

Step 8: Redefine the survey and work out any problems or mistakes.
You should do this in order to minimise any errors.

Step 9: Determine an appropriate sample.
What is your sample size? Sample fraction? The response rate? How can the sample be made representative of the population?

Step 10: Encourage people to participate in the survey.
The more people participate, the more the sample is a representation of the population. Online surveys sometimes encourage people to participate by giving away prizes for participating.

Step 11: Communicate the results of the survey.
At the end of the survey, all the results should be communicated and discussed so that the organisation can implement the improvements based on the results of the survey.

Power break 1.1 GROUP WORK

Get into groups and conduct your own survey by following the eleven steps. Decide on your objectives before you choose your method of surveying. You can do the survey via a WhatsApp broadcast, Facebook Messenger, Survey Monkey or by physically going to other students at your campus with a clipboard and writing down their answers. Try to get a minimum of 10 to 15 participants.

As a group you can decide on your own set of questions. Make use of closed-ended questions. These kinds of questions need a "yes" or "no" or "true" or "false" answer.

Discuss your objectives and results with the rest of the class.

SA's top vehicle brands for customer service

28 July 2017
Buying a car should always be a pleasure. So which car manufacturers will ensure that you drive off with a smile?

It seems that German brands are ranked at the top for customers when it comes to buying a car or bakkie in South Africa, according to the 2017 Ipsos quality survey.

Audi and Volkswagen continue to lead the way in the Ipsos Competitive Customer Experience survey, covering the 2016 calendar year. Ipsos interviewed more than 22 000 customers about their purchasing and servicing experience in 2016.

German brands shine
Both Audi and Volkswagen collected Gold Awards for the Passenger Car and Light Commercial Vehicle (LCV) Purchasing Experience for the fifth year in a row. Audi also collected Gold for the fifth year for Passenger Car Servicing, while VW grabbed Gold for the second year in a row for Passenger Car Servicing.

Figure 1.9 Ipsos conducted a customer satisfaction survey.

Example 3

Below is an example of an online survey conducted about people's opinions about employment in South Africa. As you can see, most people feel that a lot of South Africans fear losing their jobs. Only 11% of the respondents said that they did not have a job.

> **Almost all working South Africans fear losing their jobs**
>
> Yes, the political uncertainty is playing havoc with the economy 78% 1518 votes
>
> ▬▬▬▬▬▬▬▬
>
> No, I work for a strong company with sound business principles 11% 220 votes
>
> ▪
>
> I don't have a job 11% 208 votes
>
> ▪

SWOT analysis

A SWOT analysis (or SWOT matrix) is another research technique to provide information and insight to an organisation's internal and external environment.

The SWOT analysis is an abbreviation for:

S: Strengths   (Internal)
W: Weaknesses   (Internal)
O: Opportunities   (External)
T: Threats   (External)

	Internal	**External**
Can be helpful	Strengths	Opportunities
Can be harmful	Weaknesses	Threats

Did you know? The origin of the SWOT analysis is not certain. Some studies credit Stanford University's Albert Humphrey. He did not claim the creation of the SWOT analysis, but he led a research project in the 1960s–1970s, which used data from a number of Fortune 500 companies.

The SWOT analysis is a research tool for management to plan and to give the organisation a competitive advantage. The SWOT analysis identifies the organisation's strong areas, weak areas, opportunities for the organisation to explore and outside threats.

Management can explore key issues by asking a number of different questions. Some examples of questions are below.

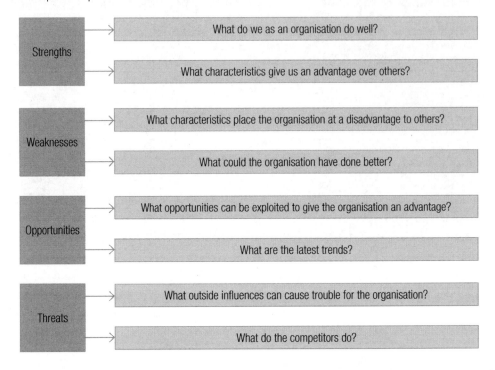

| Strengths | What do we as an organisation do well? |
| | What characteristics give us an advantage over others? |

| Weaknesses | What characteristics place the organisation at a disadvantage to others? |
| | What could the organisation have done better? |

| Opportunities | What opportunities can be exploited to give the organisation an advantage? |
| | What are the latest trends? |

| Threats | What outside influences can cause trouble for the organisation? |
| | What do the competitors do? |

It is sometimes good to assess yourself. It can be useful to be honest and to realise that you may very good in certain areas of your life, but there are also things to work on. Personality tests are part of the selection process in Module 2 and recruitment agencies conduct the same tests. In the Power break below you will do a personal SWOT analysis, which is similar to the tests recruitment agencies use.

Power break 1.2   INDIVIDUAL WORK

Everyone has a goal in life and something that they want to achieve. Do a SWOT analysis of yourself and write a report about your findings. Your assignment is a personal study and not to be discussed in class, but it will benefit you by giving you a clearer picture of where you are in life at the moment and the way forward.

Identify your own strengths and weaknesses. Be honest with yourself, and be very specific in your answers. What can you do to improve your weaknesses and further improve your strengths? Identify the opportunities for the future if you reach your goal, but also the threats that can cause conflict and cause you to not reach your goal.

Figure 1.10 Do a SWOT analysis of yourself.

UNIT 1.3 **Statistical analysis**

Data refers to information in a raw and unorganised form. It only becomes useful when this data is organised accurately and for a specific purpose.

Once data has been collected for any research project, for example, a survey or a historical study, you will have a lot of data consisting of alphabets, numbers, symbols, and so on. The next step would be to analyse that information. This is called **statistical analysis**.

> **Example 4**
>
> Go back to page 12 and read the article "SA's top vehicle brands for customer service", where Ipsos interviewed more than 22 000 customers about their purchasing and servicing experience in 2016. This mean that the data that Ipsos collected formed 22 000 different answers, or numbers.
>
> Those results, answers and numbers are data. It is raw, which means it is not organised or analysed, and therefore it does not mean anything yet.

> **DEFINITION**
>
> **statistical analysis** – a process of collecting, examining, manipulating and interpreting data with the goal of discovering useful information. Statistical analysis changes raw data into meaningful information.

Example 5

Go back to page 13 and look at the survey results in Example 3 on that page.

In total Fin24 received 1946 votes (1518 + 220 + 208). These votes are the raw and unorganised data; numbers that do not mean anything until you analyse them. In order to analyse the data, they would sort the votes for each specific category. Then they can work out the **percentage** of each category. Percentages are easy to understand and give meaningful information quickly. A percentage of 78% (1518 ÷ 1946 × 100) of the total votes means more to stakeholders than "1518 votes". When you report to stakeholders, you must remember

> **Almost all working South Africans fear losing their jobs**
>
> Yes, the political uncertainty is playing havoc with the economy 78% 1518 votes
>
> No, I work for a strong company with sound business principles 11% 220 votes
>
> I don't have a job 11% 208 votes

they do not have the background of the research and they want to receive information in a practical form.

Note that this information is presented in a horizontal bar graph. You will learn more about bar graphs in Unit 1.4.

Statistical analysis is a process of collecting, examining, manipulating and interpreting data with the goal of discovering useful information. Statistical analysis changes raw data into meaningful information.

With this useful information the organisation can make conclusions, discover causes and trends, and it will help support decision-making.

Averages and medians

The **average** refers to the sum of the numbers divided by how many numbers are being considered (how many numbers are averaged).

Averages are helpful when conducting a statistical analysis. To work out an average is to make data useful. We use averages in many different ways. In a classroom environment, for example, you want to see how your test results compare with the rest of the class. For that you need to work out the class average. Once you know the class average, you can compare your results with the average result of the class.

A lecturer can use a line graph to show the test result's averages of the past years or the average rainfall over the last five years.

> **DEFINITIONS**
>
> **percentage** – a mathematical term used to express a number as a fraction out of one hundred
> **average** – the sum of the numbers divided by how many numbers are being considered

Case study

Cape Town starts average speed testing

13 October 2014

The City of Cape Town has revealed a new weapon in the endless war against drivers who speed.

The system is about to go into operation on Nelson Mandela Boulevard in the city centre. It has quite a long name: Average Speed Over Distance Cameras.

Basically, your car is identified by its number plate as it enters the highway and again at points along it. A computer instantly calculates every vehicle's average speed and, if it's higher than the speed limit, you will be hit with a fine.

Smile for the camera! Cape Town will start shooting with its new camera traps that measure average speed over distance before the end of this month.

Figure 1.11 Average speed enforcement may result in more speeding fines for careless drivers.

The median has a similar function to the average. The **median** is the middle number in a group of numbers.

How do we calculate the median? First you sort the numbers from the highest to the lowest or lowest to the highest. Then you find the number that lies in the middle.

Example 6

You were given the following numbers: 12, 5, 8, 1 and 10.

1. Sort the numbers. 1, 5, 8, 10, 12 or 12, 10, 8, 5, 1
2. Find the middle number. The middle number is 8.
   8 is the median.

If there are two middle numbers (a middle pair), you find the value that is half way between them.

Example:

You were given the following numbers: 12, 5, 8, 1, 10 and 14.

1. Sort the numbers. 1, 5, 8, 10, 12, 14 or 14, 12, 10, 8, 5, 1
2. Number 8 and 10 are the middle pair. To find the value half way between them, you add the two numbers and divide the answer by two.
   $(8 + 10) \div 2 = 9$
   9 is the median.

Example 7

The table below shows the total number of days employees are absent per month. Calculate the average and median by using the data in the table.

Month	Days	Month	Days
January	2	July	12
February	2	August	11
March	4	September	8
April	6	October	6
May	10	November	4
June	10	December	2

Average: Find the sum of the numbers divided by how many numbers are being considered.
1. $(2 + 2 + 4 + 6 + 10 + 10 + 12 + 11 + 8 + 6 + 4 + 2) \div 12 = $ **6.4**

Median: Sort the numbers, either from lowest to highest or from highest to lowest.
1. 2, 2, 2, 4, 4, 6, 6, 8, 10, 10, 11, 12 (lowest to highest)
2. The middle number is 6. $(6 + 6) \div 2 = $ **6**

DEFINITION

median – the middle number of a list of numbers.

What is the difference between an average and median? In this example the median tells us that for half of the year employees were absent less than 6 days and for the other half of the year, employees were absent for more than 6 days. Half of the year the result is good (less than 6 days), but the other half is too high. The average absent days per month (6.4) is also a concern. This will influence the overall productivity of the department.

Percentages

A percentage (%) is a number or ratio expressed as a portion out of 100. You can convert a percentage to a fraction or express a percentage as a decimal.

We use percentages, fractions and decimals in our everyday life. The result of your test is expressed as a percentage (78%). The sale at your local supermarket is expressed as a percentage (less 30%). Your cool drink bottle is marked with a decimal (1.5 litre) and the newspaper will use a fraction to say the dams in the Western Cape are half full (½).

See Table 1.3 for the conversion of some common percentages to fractions and decimals.

Table 1.3 Percentage conversions to fractions and decimals

Percentage	Fraction	Decimal
25%	¼	0.25
50%	½	0.50
80%	⅘	0.80

Figure 1.12 Percentages are common mathematical symbols in everyday life.

If you want to represent a percentage you can do this using a pie chart or a bar graph. These are static values that do not change over time. You will learn more about pie charts and bar graphs in Unit 1.4.

The pie chart in Figure 1.13 shows the statistics for workforce at management level percentages in South Africa by race.

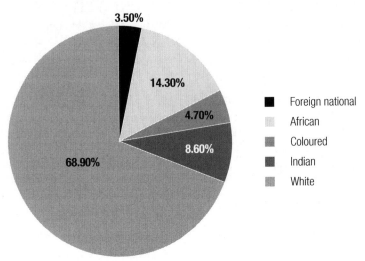

Figure 1.13 A pie chart showing stats for workforce percentages at management level by race in SA

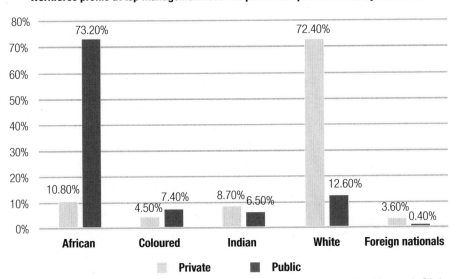

Figure 1.14 A bar graph showing stats for workforce percentages at management level by race in SA, in the private and public sector

Trends and regressions

A trend is a general direction in a series of data points on a graph. For example, a trend is the general direction of the price of an asset, whether it is becoming more or less expensive. Trends can also apply to interest rates.

Trends can also be seen in the fashion industry and in the latest developments of technology, accessories and toys. Owning the latest cell phone, computer or new invention (like a fidget spinner) would be considered "following the trend".

Figure 1.15 Trends are shown by the general direction for data points on a graph. Trends also refer to fashion trends, and things that become popular with time.

Regression is a statistical tool used to estimate the strength and the direction of the relationship between two linearly-related variables. A regression will investigate the relationship between two variables: the "independent" variable (which is known and remains constant) and the "dependent" variable (which is unknown and changes). Usually, the investigator seeks to find the effect of one variable upon another.

Linear regression is a good way to make observations and interpret data. Usually, trends and regressions would be shown on a line graph. You will learn more about line graphs in Unit 1.4

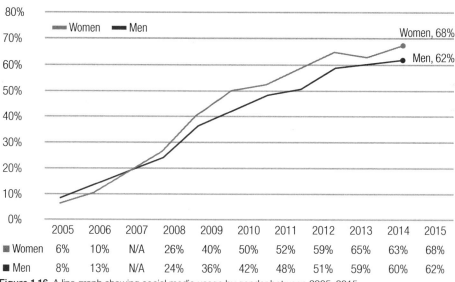

Social media adoption trends by gender

	2005	2006	2007	2008	2009	2010	2011	2012	2013	2014	2015
Women	6%	10%	N/A	26%	40%	50%	52%	59%	65%	63%	68%
Men	8%	13%	N/A	24%	36%	42%	48%	51%	59%	60%	62%

Figure 1.16 A line graph showing social media usage by gender between 2005–2015

DEFINITIONS

trends – the general direction in a series of data points on a graph

regressions – the statistical tools used to estimate the strength and the direction of the relationship between two linearly related variables

Example 8

Thuli is a scientist studying the time management and study skills of college students. She conducts an experiment at a local college with 20 students. She asks each student to track their average time spent on social media for a month. This will be the known variable (the independent variable), because the average time spent on social media stays more or less the same.

She also asks them to record their test mark at the end of the month. This will be the unknown variable (the dependent variable). Students do not know their mark beforehand and it is seldom the same.

Once all 20 students turn in their data, Thuli creates a scatterplot, which is a graph of ordered pairs showing a relationship between the two sets of data (time spent on social media and test result).

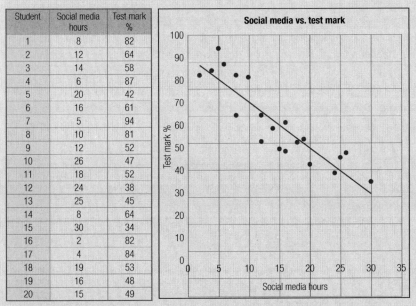

Student	Social media hours	Test mark %
1	8	82
2	12	64
3	14	58
4	6	87
5	20	42
6	16	61
7	5	94
8	10	81
9	12	52
10	26	47
11	18	52
12	24	38
13	25	45
14	8	64
15	30	34
16	2	82
17	4	84
18	19	53
19	16	48
20	15	49

Figure 1.17 Thuli's scatterplot showing the correlation between social media usage and test results

Thuli finds a regression line by drawing a line that is closest to as many points as possible. The regression line is a straight line that attempts to predict the relationship between two points.

With Thuli's research, you can see the relationship between time spent on social media and the test marks. From the graph you can see that the students with the highest test marks are the ones that spend the least amount of time on social media.

Indexes

Indexes are a way to determine how much something has changed over a period of time. On the stock exchange, indexes are used to show the overall performance of a particular stock. A stock index, or stock market index, is a measurement of a section of the stock market that is calculated according to the price of different stocks. Statistics South Africa is an agency that officially keeps this information.

For example, the Johannesburg Stock Exchange (JSE) includes 150+ listed companies. If you check the "all share index" you can see the day's and the year's overall performance for all the listed companies. This number can then be compared to individual companies.

Figure 1.18 The stock exchange relies on indexes to measure changes in the value of certain stocks.

Ratios

A **ratio** is the relationship between two numbers. The relationship is usually shown with a colon in the middle, for example, 1:2. If you need to dilute your juice with six times as much water than concentrate, it might say "dilute 1:6" on the bottle. You also might have seen this on maps or model cars.

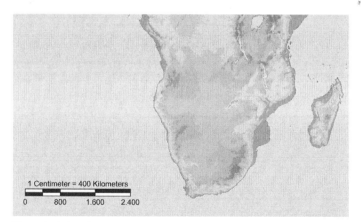

Figure 1.19 A scale on a map shows the ratio of centimetres to kilometres.

> **DEFINITION**
>
> **ratio** – the relationship between two numbers. A ratio indicates how many times one number contains another number.

This map shows scale, which indicates that 1 centimetre is equal to 400 kilometres. This could be expressed as 1cm : 400km.

Another example would be the ratio of male to female students in your class. Say for instance the ratio is 20:32, which means there are 20 male and 32 female students in this class of 52. You can simplify the ratio by dividing both by the common denominator, 20. The ratio can then be written as 1:1.6.

UNIT 1.4 **Graphic representations**

People understand information better when they can see it visually. Graphs and charts are graphic representations of data. With graphs and charts, you can see comparisons, trends and regressions. Microsoft Excel is one programme you can use to create data charts.

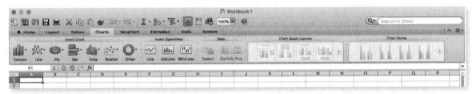

Figure 1.20 The chart tool in Microsoft Excel

Different types of graphs

Line graphs

A line graph is a graphical device that displays information as a series of data connected by straight line segments. This is the most basic and versatile chart, and is the most frequently used form of chart. You can use a line graph when working with percentages or raw data numbers of whatever you are measuring, for example, the number of people, the temperature in degrees or the height in metres.

The line graph works on a horizontal and vertical axis. The horizontal axis (x-axis, left to right) usually shows time. The vertical axis (y-axis, upright) shows variable data, for example, numbers or percentages. The line joins points on the graph where the x-axis and y-axis meet, showing how the variable increased or decreased over time.

When to use a line graph

Line graphs are used to track changes over periods of time. When smaller changes exist, line graphs are better to use than bar graphs because it is easier to see a small change on a line graph.

Line graphs can also be used to compare changes over the same period of time for more than one group. For example, the human resources department can use the averages of the staff turnover over the last five years and plot that on a line graph. When the human resources manager discusses staff turnover with the board of directors, they can visually see if there is an increase (going up) or a decrease (going down) in the number of people leaving the organisation and the number of people being appointed every year.

This will give the board of directors a visual on the trends (the dotted line) over the last few years as well. Positive trends show that staff turnover decreased over time; negative trends show that the staff turnover increased.

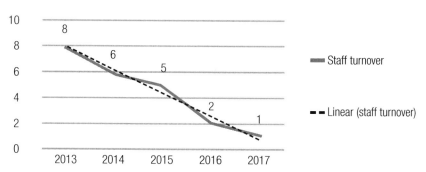

Staff turnover

Figure 1.21 A line graph showing a positive trend in staff turnover between 2013 and 2017

Power break 1.3   INDIVIDUAL WORK

Use the line graph to answer the questions below.

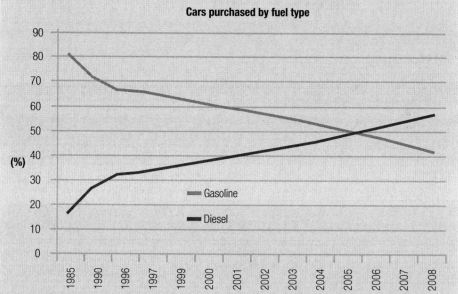

Cars purchased by fuel type

Figure 1.22 A simple line graph showing the percentage of cars purchased by fuel type (gasoline or diesel) between 1985 and 2008

1 In which year were the most diesel cars purchased?
2 In which year were the least diesel cars purchased?
3 In which year were the same number of diesel and gasoline cars purchased?
4 What is the general trend?

Bar graphs

A bar graph (also called a bar chart) is a chart that uses either horizontal or vertical bars to show you how different categories of data compare. There are different types of bar charts: vertical bar graphs and horizontal bar graphs.

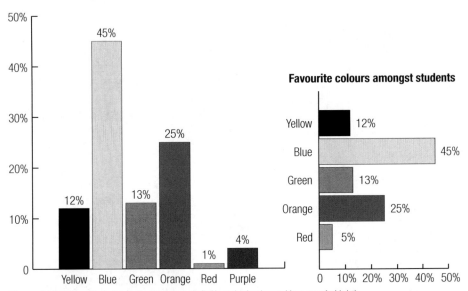

Figure 1.23 Examples of a vertical bar graph (left) and a horizontal bar graph (right)

When to use a bar graph

Bar graphs are used to compare things between different groups or to track changes over time. However, when trying to measure changes over time, bar graphs are best when the changes are larger. Use a line graph for smaller changes as they are difficult to see on a bar graph.

For example, if the human resources department wants to compare the number of men versus women in the organisation over the last five years, they should use a bar graph. They may want to use the ratio of men versus woman for their equity report, which would show a figure for men and women, for example, 15:19 in 2017. That means there are 19 women for every 15 men in the company.

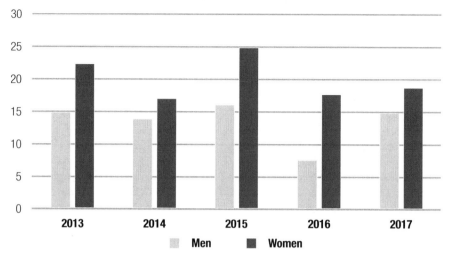

Figure 1.24 A vertical bar graph showing the number of men and women in an organisation between 2013 and 2017

Pie charts

A pie chart is a circular graphic that shows percentages or proportional data. The circle is divided into slices to illustrate the proportions, just like how you might cut up a pie. All the percentages in a pie chart must add up to 100%.

The pie chart in Figure 1.25 shows the results of a survey to see which colour students like best. You can clearly see that the biggest slice of the pie is for the colour blue. This means that the highest percentage of students like the colour blue (45%). This means blue is the most popular colour. Orange is the second most popular; green is the third most popular; yellow is the fourth most popular colour; and red is the least popular colour.

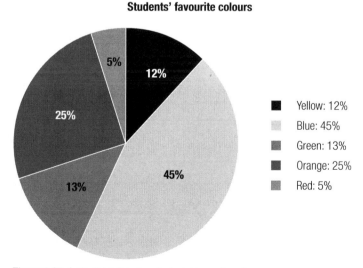

Figure 1.25 A pie chart showing students' favourite colours

Example 9

You conduct a survey with your friends to find the kind of movie they like best:

Favourite type of movie				
Comedy	Action	Romance	Drama	SciFi
4	5	6	1	4

Favourite movie type

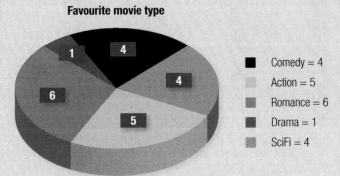

Comedy = 4
Action = 5
Romance = 6
Drama = 1
SciFi = 4

Figure 1.26 A pie chart showing favourite type of movie

It is easy to see which movie is most liked, and which one is the least popular.

* Most popular = Romance (30%)
* Least popular = Drama (5%)

To calculate the percentage:

* There were 20 participants in total.
* 4 of the 20 like comedy the most.
* $4 \div 20 \times 100 = 20\%$
* The total of all the percentages will always be 100%.

When to use a pie chart

Pie charts are best to use when you are trying to compare parts of a whole. Pie charts are not useful for showing changes over time. The human resources manager of a firm might use a pie chart to show the percentages of the labour cost for each department in the organisation. As you can see in the pie chart below, in this particular organisation the largest percentage goes to Finance (36%).

Division of the labour budget by department

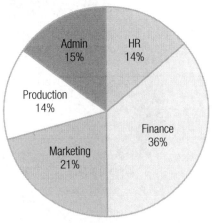

Figure 1.27 A pie chart showing the division of the labour budget by department

WHAT DO WE KNOW AND WHERE TO NEXT...

Revisiting the learning objectives

Now that you have completed this module you should have achieved the learning objectives listed in the table below:

Learning objective	What you have learned	Tick box
Give reasons why personnel research must be conducted in practice.	The reasons why personnel research must be conducted in practice: • Recruitment of employees • Training and development • Compensation/rewards for employees • Maintaining employee relations • Separation.	☐
Explain different research methods and instruments to be used when conducting research in practice.	The two types of research: • Basic (exploratory) • Applied (operational).	☐
	The different research methods: • Historical studies • Case Studies • Role play • Simulation • Field Study • Laboratory Experiments • Aggregate Quantitative Reviews.	☐
Explain briefly the procedure to be used when conducting research by referring to the steps to be taken in getting a project under way.	The procedure to be used when conducting a research project (steps): Step 1: Define research problem Step 2: Describe the objective(s) for the research Step 3: Decide on the research method Step 4: Collect the information Step 5: Analyse and process the data Step 6: Interpret the data Step 7: Compile a report Step 8: Propose possible ways to solve the problem.	☐
Demonstrate practically (in steps) how to do a survey.	Steps in conducting a survey: Step 1: Formulate the survey Step 2: Determine the procedures you want to follow Step 3: Describe the plan for the survey	☐

Learning objective	What you have learned	Tick box
	Step 4: Analyse each question	
	Step 5: Decide on the specific order of the questions	
	Step 6: Determine the standard for the survey	
	Step 7: Give clear instructions on how to complete the survey	
	Step 8: Redefine the survey and work out any problems or mistakes	
	Step 9: Determine an appropriate sample	
	Step 10: Encourage people to participate in the survey	
	Step 11: Communicate the results of the survey.	
Prepare an elementary SWOT analysis in practice.	The SWOT-analysis: • Strengths • Weaknesses • Opportunities • Threats.	☐
Statistical analysis	See Unit 1.3 (p. 16): • Averages • Medians • Percentages • Trends • Regressions • Indexes • Ratios	☐
Assess graphic representations as used in personnel practice.	Understand and know when to use each of the following types of graphic representations: • Line graphs • Bar graphs • Pie charts.	☐

Assessment

True or false
Choose whether the following statements are TRUE or FALSE. Write only the number of the question followed by 'true' or 'false'.

1. Surveys, observations and screening are personnel research methods.
2. The value of a well-conducted survey as a personnel research method is that it helps to obtain data that is accurate, valid and reliable.
3. Validity means the survey measures what it is supposed to measure.
4. Historical studies are also known as field studies.
5. Personnel research uses information obtained to manage people effectively.

(5 × 2) [10]

Multiple choice questions

Choose the correct answer from the various options provided. Choose only A, B, C or D and write your answer next to the question number.

1. Which of the following is not part of reward management? (2)
    A   Adjusting to inflation
    B   Fringe benefits
    C   Determining the success of training
    D   Paying the employee a bonus

2. What is the last step in a research project? (2)
    A   To compile a report
    B   To communicate the results to everyone involved
    C   To interpret the data
    D   To propose a solution to solve the problem

3. _____ means a survey will have the same result regardless of who conducts it. (2)
    A   Reliability
    B   Validity
    C   Consistency
    D   Accuracy

4. The common fraction % is equal to: (2)
    A   4:8
    B   0.70
    C   75%
    D   ½

5. The results of a mathematics competition are: 78.5%, 80.1%, 68.3%, 47.2% and 88.9%. Determine the average and median. (2)
    A   Average – 72.6%   Median – 80.1%
    B   Average – 74.2%   Median – 72.6%
    C   Average – 80.1%   Median – 74.2%
    D   Average – 72.6%   Median – 74.2%   (5 × 2) [10]

Short questions

Briefly answer the following questions:

1. Explain the need for personnel research. (6)
2. Name the five areas of personnel research from a manager's perspective. (5)
3. Explain the following personnel research methods:
    a) Field study (4)
    b) Laboratory experiments. (6)
4. Explain what personnel research is. (4)
5. Name the two types of research. (2)
6. What is statistical analysis? (3)
                                                                              [30]

Long questions

Answer the following questions as comprehensively as you can:

1. Name the EIGHT basic steps that comprise the research process.   (8 × 2)
2. Name the EIGHT different research methods.   (8)
3. Calculate the median and average time of an athletics competition by using the results given in the following table: (5 × 2)

100m FINAL			
Athlete	**Time**	**Athlete**	**Time**
John Peters	9.85 s	Mike Smith	10.65 s
Koos Meyer	10.00 s	Jonathan September	9.98 s
Abrie Demper	10.70 s	Keegan Nield	10.60 s
Xola Mbasa	9.95 s	Eric Smuts	10.11 s

4. What are the differences between accuracy and reliability?   (4)
5. Name the ELEVEN steps involved in conducting a survey.   (11 × 2)

[60]

Grand total: 110 marks

HUMAN RESOURCE PROVISION

This module covers the following:

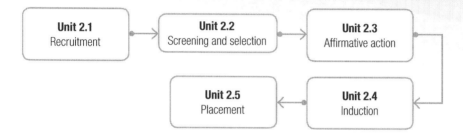

| Unit 2.1 Recruitment | Unit 2.2 Screening and selection | Unit 2.3 Affirmative action |

| Unit 2.5 Placement | Unit 2.4 Induction |

Learning objectives

By the end of this module, you should be able to do the following:
* Explain briefly what is meant by recruitment in work practice
* Describe in a pragmatic way the importance of a recruitment policy
* Indicate which factors influence recruitment in an organisation in the South African context
* Identify internal and external sources of recruitment and the practical implications thereof
* Use recruitment processes as applicable in the South African work environment
* Discuss how and why the recruitment process of an organisation is evaluated for effectiveness in practice
* Explain briefly what is meant by screening and selection in the personnel recruitment practice
* Identify which factors of the internal and external environment affect the screening of candidates
* Demonstrate the steps in the screening process in a pragmatic way
* Differentiate between different screening techniques
* Demonstrate how to conduct interviews in the screening process to ensure effective selection in practice
* Describe the measures used to evaluate the screening and selection process
* Describe the meaning of affirmative action as a strategy in the recruitment process and the practical implications thereof

- Discuss affirmative action as a means of employee development in the South African work environment
- Explain briefly the formulation and implementation of affirmative action in practice
- Explain briefly what is meant by placement as part of personnel recruitment practice
- Describe the aim of placement in the work environment
- Differentiate between different placement strategies in practice
- Explain the different methods or techniques for placement which are currently applied in the work environment
- Explain what is meant by induction
- Discuss the aim of effective induction in the work environment
- Explain in a pragmatic way the different components of an induction programme, including general orientation of the new employee
- Explain how and why evaluation of the induction process of an organisation is done.

Key terms

affirmative action	induction	recruitment
demotion	placement	reliability
discrimination	policy	transfer
employment	promotion	validity

Starting point

Julian is the human resources manager at a motor tracking firm, and he and his manager did some research as discussed in Module 1. The motor tracking industry is growing day by day because of the high demand. According to their research and analysis, their company is doing very well. In fact, his manager wants to expand the business by opening another branch.

Julian's manager wants to transfer her assistant manager to the new branch to be the manager. The assistant manager's position will be advertised internally. Julian and the human resources department's first goal is to fill the position with a current employee who meets the necessary qualifications and competencies before they advertise externally.

The trade union is very happy with Julian and the company's decision to transfer the assistant manager and fill his position from within the company. The company is committed to their employment equity plan and will take that into consideration when appointing the new assistant manager.

Figure 2.1 Julian and his manager will start interviewing new candidates soon.

UNIT 2.1 Recruitment

Human resource management (HRM) is the management of an organisation's interplay with the work and the people who do the work. Human resource management is responsible for managing the human resources effectively for an organisation to reach their goal. Recruitment is one of the activities of the human resource management department.

What is recruitment?

Recruitment is often seen as simply the process of filling vacant positions within the organisation. However, recruitment is much more than that. Recruitment involves a high degree of planning in order to ensure that the organisation attracts and retains the most suitable candidates who will successfully contribute towards the organisation's objectives.

Recruitment is the cost effective search for people who have the necessary potential, knowledge, skills and abilities to fill positions as employees who will assist the organisation in achieving its objectives. Effective recruitment matches the ability and behavior of the best possible candidates with the ability and behavior required for a position.

The aim of recruitment includes:

- Identifying that a job vacancy exists
- Identifying the need to fill the vacancy
- Attracting the best possible candidates to apply for the vacancy
- Creating a positive image of the organisation that will attract potential candidates
- Maintaining adequate supply of employees with the necessary skills and abilities to help the organisation reach their goals
- Making an informed decision about who is to fill the position successfully
- Ensuring the organisation does not miss out on any opportunities to recruit quality candidates.

Did you know? According to Dr. Pierre Mornell, the author of *45 Effective Ways for Hiring Smart*, if you make a mistake in hiring, and you recognise and rectify the mistake within six months, the cost of replacing that employee is two and a half times the person's annual salary.

Key point: Recruitment involves planning to ensure that the organisation attracts and retains the most suitable candidates.

DEFINITION

recruitment – the cost effective search for people who have the necessary potential, knowledge, skills and abilities to fill positions as employees within an organisation

Recruitment policy

In general, a **policy** states what the company does and how it deals with particular issues. A policy is very specific and binding to everyone in the organisation. The recruitment policy is a document that stipulates detailed guidelines on how an organisation deals with recruitment. It explains exactly what needs to be done during and after the recruitment process.

The recruitment policy makes the process consistent and fair to everyone, and it guides the recruitment process. The policy also spells out exactly who is responsible for every step of the recruitment process. There are other important aspects to be considered in the recruitment policy, such as:

- The legal prescriptions regarding fairness and **discrimination**. The policy should adhere to all legislation in South Africa (the Labour Relations Act, **Employment** Equity Act, Basic Conditions of Employment Act, etc.)
- The recruitment budget limitations
- The clauses in the collective agreements with trade unions
- The way the organisation functions
- The structure and the way communication lines of authority work, as well as leadership styles.

The purpose of this policy is to support the design and implementation of the organisation's recruitment practices.

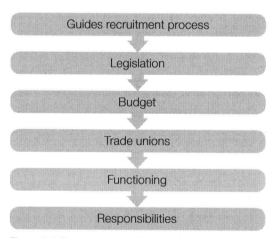

Figure 2.2 The key aspects of the recruitment policy

DEFINITIONS

policy – the broad guidelines of an organisation

discrimination – the unfair treatment of a person (or a group of people) based on their skin colour, sex, religion, etc.

employment – the hiring of an individual to provide an organisation with their time, skills and services in exchange for compensation

Guidelines for recruitment

It is important for organisations to have guidelines for recruitment. These will vary depending on the organisation itself, and each organisation can alter the guidelines to best fit their needs, work environment and industry. The list below is an example of general guidelines to follow:

- Formulate a recruitment policy. Consult with top management
- Recruitment and selection policy and procedures are subject to current legislation and the organisation should consult with the Department of Labour for guidance
- Make sure the recruitment process is cost effective
- Each position advertised should represent a real and currently available job
- Review the position description to determine if any changes or updates should be made to the position
- Do not use offensive content and do not discriminate against anyone
- Determine what legal prescriptions should be taken into account
- Determine which clauses in collective agreements with trade unions are applicable
- Job titles should be the name of the particular position, with no unnecessary information
- Each position advertised should be authorised by the applicable manager
- Make a decision on the most appropriate method of advertising that will result in interest from suitable candidates.

Factors that influence recruitment in South Africa

Businesses in South Africa do not operate in a vacuum and are influenced by a number of external (outside the organisation) and internal (inside the organisation) factors.

External factors

- **The economy and labour market conditions**

  The country's economy plays a crucial role in terms of the state of the labour market. In a growing economy there is a usually a high demand for suitable, qualified candidates. Organisations are expanding, opening new branches and businesses can afford to appoint new employees. In times when the economy is not doing well (like a recession), the demand for new employees will be low.

- **Supply and demand**

  Supply and demand goes hand-in-hand with the economy. In South Africa there is a very high supply of unskilled and semi-skilled job seekers and a very low supply of skilled workers. When the supply is high, the recruitment effort will generate many applicants. If the supply is low, organisations have to be more creative and effort may be needed to recruit the best candidates.

- **Political and legal considerations**

  The government provides a comprehensive legislative framework, which guides the organisation's recruitment policy. This framework of laws and regulations are there to protect both the employer and future candidate's rights. Some Acts of Parliament that affect recruitment are the Labour Relations Act (LRA), No. 66 of 1995, the Employment Equity Act, No 55 of 1998, the Basic Conditions of Employment Act 1997, and so on.

- **Affirmative action**

  The purpose of the Employment Equity Act, No 55 of 1998, is to achieve equity in the workplace by promoting equal opportunities and fair treatment in employment. It applies to all employers and workers and protects workers and job seekers from unfair discrimination, and also provides a framework for implementing **affirmative action**. This will be discussed in detail in Unit 2.3.

- **Trade unions**

  Trade unions represent employees in a particular organisation. The unions' goals are to reduce industrial relations conflicts, eliminate unfair discrimination and redress past discrimination in the workplace.

- **The technological environment**

  Technology is very dynamic. With the internet, social media and high-tech applicant tracking systems, it continuously influences the way organisations recruit.

- **The image of the organisation**

  The image of an organisation influences future applicants' perceptions of the company. A positive image will attract a large number of applications, but the opposite can also apply. With social media being so prolific, it is important to maintain a positive image. Often, it is not the money that is important. It is the perception of the company that matters in attracting qualified prospective employees.

Power break 2.1   GROUP DISCUSSION

A prestigious UK based public relations firm, Bell Pottinger, was involved in a PR campaign in South Africa in 2016/2017 that caused a lot of damage to their reputation.

1 Do some research on what happened and discuss in groups how you think the scandal negatively affected their reputation. Consider the image of the company and their ability to recruit the best people in future.
2 Think of a South African company that has a positive image. What are your reasons for saying so?

Internal factors

- **The recruitment policy of the organisation**

  As discussed before, the recruitment policy is a document that stipulates broad guidelines on how an organisation deals with recruitment. It explains exactly what needs to be done for recruitment in an organisation and who is responsible. The policy will also determine the type of people chosen to work in the organisation.

DEFINITION

affirmative action – the labour policy aimed at redressing the inequalities of the past and, in so doing, achieving a transformed workplace, which is representative of the greater South Africa

---

- **The cost of recruitment**

  Recruitment can be very expensive and recruiters must operate within budgets. This money is then used to place adverts, interview candidates (which may involve paying their travel costs), use recruitment resources, and train new employees.

- **The organisational culture**

  In South Africa we have many different cultures, languages, values and customs. An organisation can also have its own culture. This includes the way they do things, their values, customs and norms. A new applicant does not only need the necessary qualifications and experience, but also has to fit in with the organisation's culture.

- **The recruitment standards**

  An organisation expects a new employee to be able to meet the necessary standards for production or service delivery set by the organisation. The human resources department needs to find candidates who are qualified for the role that has been advertised, so that new employees are able to meet these standards.

- **The size of the organisation**

  The recruitment process is affected by the size of the organisation. Usually larger organisations recruit more candidates than small ones.

Sources of recruitment

There are two sources of recruitment; external and internal. External recruitment is when the business looks to fill the vacancy from any suitable applicant outside the business. Internal recruitment is when the business looks to fill the vacancy from within its existing workforce.

Table 2.1 Sources of recruitment

External resources	Internal resources
Advertisement – direct applications	**Promotion**
E-recruitment	**Transfer**
Private employment agencies	Word of mouth
Public employment agencies	Internal employee referral/recommendation
Campus recruitment	Internal advertising (present database)
Recommendations/referrals	Notice boards
Head hunters	
Walk-ins	
Temporary employees	

DEFINITIONS

promotion – the most common form of internal recruitment where an employee is moved to an upper level of the organisation with more responsibility and prestige

transfer – the horizontal movement of an employee between departments or branches

External recruitment

Let us look at the following sources of external recruitment, as well as some advantages and disadvantages.

- **Advertisements**

  Responding to advertisements is one of the most common methods of applying for a job. Direct applications eliminate any middlemen in the process of sourcing new talent for an organisation. The organisation advertises by using print media, electronic media, or both.

Figure 2.3 An example of a job advertisement in print

Power break 2.2   INDIVIDUAL WORK

A good and well-planned advertisement needs to meet certain requirements or criteria. Study and evaluate the print advertisement below by rating each criterion of the advertisement and answering the questions. Rate by ticking (✓) in the appropriate box (1 = very poor or not meeting the criteria, 2 = average, 3 = good, 4 = very good or 5 = excellent).

to be continued...

DEFINITIONS

print media – text and images printed on paper, such as newspapers, magazines, printed journals and pamphlets

electronic media – ways of sharing information that are not in print, such as radio, television, and the internet

AMPHIBIAN MEDIA

Multimedia Reporter
Frog News

Frog News Network has an exciting vacancy for a multimedia reporter. The successful applicant will be responsible for producing copy across multiple platforms in a variety of media (print and digital).

Key responsibilities:

- Produce high-quality news stories that are error-free and print ready
- Produce regular front page leads
- Produce regular feature articles
- Establish a strong network of contacts
- Edit copy to comply with legal, space and style requirements
- Manage a personal diary
- Initiate stories.

Minimum requirements:

- A tertiary qualification in journalism or similar field
- At least 3 years journalism experience working on multiple platforms
- Must have a strong presence on social media
- Valid driver's licence.

Required competencies:

- Must be technologically well-advanced on all social media platforms
- Excellent interpersonal skills, including ability to deal with high profile contacts
- Must have the ability to think creatively
- Must be highly flexible working long, irregular hours, including nightshift
- Must be prepared to travel long distances across the province and the country
- Must be prepared to work under constant pressure of tight deadlines.

Frog News Network is committed to its employment equity and affirmative action plan.

All applicants should submit a written CV and covering letter by 12 August 2019 to:

Rachel Mkize
Frog News
Lily Pad Close
22 Ribbit Street

Email: r.mkize@frognews.co.za

to be continued...

CRITERIA	1	2	3	4	5
Presentation:					
General appearance					
Layout					
Creative design (visually stimulating)					
Font and font sizes					
Content:					
Mentions the name of the vacancy					
Mentions the name of the organisation					
States the minimum requirements and qualifications					
States the remuneration, benefits, working conditions on offer					
States how the applicant should apply for the position					
States the closing date for applicants					
States the organisation's commitment to employment equity					
Target Market:					
Attracts the attention of suitable applicants only					

Questions:

1 What is your overall view of this advertisement? Which box did you tick (✓) the most?
2 Would you have applied for this position if you had the necessary skills and qualifications?
3 What would you change or add to make this advertisement better?

- **E-recruitment**

  E-recruitment is also known as online recruitment. Online recruitment reduces the administrative and financial burden of recruitment and helps an organisation to gain access to a wider pool of talent. Organisations may choose to advertise on their own website or post the position on a careers website.

Did you know? There are websites dedicated to job listings. Organisations can advertise there to a broad potential employee base and applicants can choose from a variety of jobs. Some examples are: www.careers24.com, www.indeed.co.za, www.careerjunction.co.za.

- **Private employment agencies**

  A private employment agency is an organisation that matches employers to employees. They interview job-seekers and keep their CVs on a database (file) until an organisation approaches them to find a specific candidate with specific qualifications and experience to fill a position.

- **Public employment agencies**

  A public employment agency is one that specialises in sourcing applicants for government vacancies (public sector).

- **Campus recruitment**

  Campus recruitment is when a company has a strategy that involves filling a certain number of jobs or internship slots with candidates from a specific campus or educational institution.

- **Recommendations/referrals**

  Current employees recommend a person (friend, family member or someone they met or know of) to fill a specific vacancy. The disadvantage is that some fellow employees might not be in favour of an employee referral program, feeling it shows bias, favouritism or nepotism. The advantages are that an organisation can save recruitment costs and that someone can vouch for a high-quality candidate.

- **Head hunters**

  This refers to a specialised recruitment agency that identifies, tracks and approaches highly qualified candidates to fill senior-level and executive jobs.

- **Walk-ins**

  A lot of companies these days entertain walk-in interviews where candidates can simply reach the office, and be interviewed by the employer on a specified date and time. Walk-in interviews give opportunities to a lot of people to apply and be interviewed. It also saves the company time when they are in urgent need of conducting a process with many people. Sending your CV to the human resources department or manager via email or fax can also be seen as a walk-in.

- **Temporary employees**

  Some individuals are hired to help the organisation meet an increased short term demand for its products or services. Students who work during holidays are an example of temporary employees. These employees do not have the status of permanent staff. Temporary employment may be a win-win situation for both the organisation and employee. A temporary employee who demonstrates a good work ethic, fits the company culture, learns quickly, regularly lends a helping hand, and does not need a manager to tell them what to do next, may receive an offer of employment.

Power break 2.3   INDIVIDUAL WORK

Choose the external recruitment source from COLUMN B to match the position mentioned in COLUMN A. Write only the letter next to the question number.

COLUMN A		COLUMN B	
1.	Online job advertisement	A	Private employment agencies
2.	Current employees vouch for a friend	B	Walk-ins
3.	DHET Lecturer	C	Recommendations/referrals
4.	Visiting City College to meet students	D	Temporary employees
5.	Finding an interviewed candidate on a system/database	E	Head hunters
6.	No open, advertised vacancy	F	Campus recruitment
7.	Students working during the holiday	G	Public employment agencies
8.	Searching for a specific, high profile person to fill the vacancy.	H	E-recruitment

External recruitment	
Advantages	**Disadvantages**
• New employees from outside bring 'new blood' into the organisation in the form of new ideas, competencies and potential. They will bring a fresh and new way of doing things. • Looking outside for new employees will give the organsation a larger pool of workers from which to find the best candidate.	• There is the real possibility that the new employee may not fit in with the organisation's culture, which can have a negative effect. • Employing candidates from outside may create a negative attitude and resentment towards them from the current employees. • Initially, new employees will not be as productive as current employees. New employees still need to find their feet in the organisation. • To go through the advertising, interviewing, assessing and **induction** process is time consuming. • The cost to appoint candidates from outside is much more expensive. The organisation incurs high costs in the advertising, interviewing, assessing and induction process.

Internal recruitment

Now let us look at the internal sources of recruitment and their advantages and disadvantages.

• **Promotion**

Promotion is the most common form of internal recruitment. Employees are moved to the upper levels of the organisation with more responsibility and prestige.

Figure 2.4 Getting a promotion can be very motivational for employees.

DEFINITION

induction – the process of welcoming and receiving the new employee to the organisation and preparing them for their new role

- **Transfer**

  Transfer means an employee is moved from one job to another, or one branch to another. Typically, the job is of a similar nature, without any change in rank and responsibility. The purpose of transfer is to enable the employee to get well-acquainted with all aspects of the organisation, which is essential for promotion in the future.

- **Internal advertising (emails, newsletters, forms)**

  This is when the human resources department uses their present database to fill a vacancy by advertising inside the organisation itself. They will look for candidates with the necessary skills, abilities, experience or potential.

- **Word of mouth**

  Word of mouth is when things are communicated from one person to another in an informal setting. Usually this means that current employees might tell their colleagues about an open vacancy inside the organisation.

- **Internal employee referral/recommendation**

  This happens when human resources can identify potential candidates from their existing employees' social networks. It is one of the most credible forms of internal recruitment because the person puts their reputation on the line every time they make a recommendation or referral and that person has nothing to gain but the appreciation of the employee's skills, ability, knowledge and experience.

- **Notice boards**

  A notice board in the office can be one constructive method of promoting important information like open vacancies to a large number of people.

Internal recruitment	
Advantages	**Disadvantages**
• It is cheaper and quicker to recruit from within the organisation. • Existing personnel are already familiar with the business, how it operates and the organisation's culture. Existing staff can be productive from day one. • Providing opportunities for promotion within the business can be motivating for staff. It will be seen as a reward for your hard work and loyalty to the organisation. • The business already knows the strengths and weaknesses of candidates. Strengths can be used to the maximum and the organisation can help to improve staff's weaknesses with training and courses.	• The organisation may lose the opportunity to employ good, new candidates from outside the organisation. • The organisation may lose the opportunity to introduce new and innovative ideas from outside. • Employing current staff may cause a feeling of resentment amongst those staff members who are candidates who were not appointed. • Appointing current staff creates another vacancy somewhere else in the organisation that needs to be filled. • Promoted employees might not rise to the challenge of the new position as expected.

Table 2.2 A comparison of external and internal recruitment

Basis for comparison	External recruitment	Internal recruitment
Meaning	Vacancy filled from any suitable applicant outside the business	Vacancy filled from within its existing workforce
Basis	Qualifications and experience	Seniority and experience
Time taken	Lengthy process	Quick process
Induction training	Essential	Not necessarily required
Cost	Costly	Cost effective
Choice of candidates	Unlimited	Limited

The recruitment process

Recruitment processes vary from company to company. The steps below apply to a general recruitment process. Each organisation might make small adjustments for their particular situation and policy.

Step 1: Identify the vacancy and evaluate the organisation's need.
Step 2: Develop a job description.
Step 3: Develop a recruitment plan.
Step 4: A selected committee makes plans on how and when to advertise the vacancy.
Step 5: Post the vacancy and implement the recruitment plan.
Step 6: Review résumés and shortlist the best applications.
Step 7: Candidates are invited for interviews and selection tests.
Step 8: Conduct face-to-face interviews.
Step 9: Prepare for the selection process.

Power break 2.4 **GROUP WORK**

Form groups of three to five members. Prepare a presentation for the class to explain the purpose of each step in the recruitment process. Table 2.3 gives you an example of how to structure your presentation.

Table 2.3 The nine steps in the recruitment process

STEPS IN THE RECRUITMENT PROCESS	THE PURPOSE OF THE STEP
Step 1: Identify the vacancy and evaluate the organisation's need.	Slide 1
Step 2: Develop a job description.	Slide 2
Step 3: Develop a recruitment plan.	Slide 3
Step 4: A selected committee makes plans on how and when to advertise the vacancy.	Slide 4
Step 5: Post the vacancy and implement the recruitment plan.	Slide 5
Step 6: Review résumés and shortlist the best applications.	Slide 6
Step 7: Candidates are invited for interviews and selection tests.	Slide 7
Step 8: Conduct face-to-face interview.	Slide 8
Step 9: Prepare for the selection process.	Slide 9

Evaluation of the recruitment process

It is very important to evaluate the organisation's recruitment process in terms of the staff turnover, speed and cost. Depending on the organisation's priorities and recruitment policy, these considerations will be different and the evaluation done at different times. The human resources department is responsible for an accurate and complete recruitment process. In smaller businesses, it is the owner or manager who would be responsible for the recruitment process.

Staff turnover

One of the best indicators to determine if the recruitment strategy is succeeding or not is the turnover of new appointments. A low **staff turnover** can be seen as good and positive, while a high staff turnover is negative and should raise concerns about the recruitment process. We are going to discuss staff turnover in detail in Module 3.

> **Did you know?** On average, 25% of new hires leave their company within the first year of coming on board. If this is happening in your organisation there may be some alarm bells ringing about the effectiveness of your recruitment process.

Speed

Part of the evaluation should involve measuring the speed of the recruitment process. This involves working out how long it takes to fill a vacancy.

Cost

The fundamental consideration when evaluating the recruitment process is the cost incurred and to compare that figure with the recruitment budget. Evaluation and feedback are necessary to determine where the organisation needs to cut costs.

> **DEFINITION**
>
> **staff turnover** – the number/percentage of employees who leave an organisation and are replaced by new employees

Did you know?

In 2016:

- 30% of people searched for new jobs while at work
- 79% of candidates were likely to use social media in their job search
- 76% of résumés were discarded for an unprofessional email address
- Over 90% of résumés were posted online or sent via email. (In 2000, only 22% of résumés were submitted via email or posted online.)
- 70% of candidates used mobile devices to find jobs.

UNIT 2.2 Screening and selection

What is screening and selection?

After the organisation has sourced **viable** candidates, the next step is to screen and select the potential candidates. Screening and selection are part of the same process.

During the **screening** stage, the organisation evaluates the applicants' qualifications and subjects them to intense scrutiny to determine which applicants are the most qualified for the position. In the screening process, candidates who do not meet the minimum requirements for the position are eliminated. For example, if the job advertisement states that the minimum requirement is Grade 12 and the applicant does not have that, they are immediately eliminated from the potential candidate list. The objective is to identify the most qualified candidates for the vacant position.

The **selection** process follows screening and it involves matching the candidate who possesses the necessary skills, experience and qualifications with the vacant position. Usually this involves some form of testing, interviewing and finally employing the successful candidate as we will discuss in detail in this unit.

Factors that affect the screening and selection process

There are internal and external factors that influence the selection process.

Internal factors

Organisations have control over the internal factors that affect their recruitment functions.

DEFINITIONS

viable – possible or likely to succeed

screening – the part of the recruitment process where candidates who do not meet the minimum requirements for the position are eliminated

selection – the process of putting the right candidate in the right position. It is a procedure of matching organisational requirements with the skills and qualifications of the potential candidate

---

The internal factors are:

Size of organisation

The size of the organisation is a factor that can affect the recruitment process. Often smaller companies will have a hiring manager who makes hiring decisions, whereas larger companies often have whole human resources departments to handle this role. The selection process of smaller organisations can be more informal whereas that of larger organisations could be more formally structured.

Recruitment policy

The recruitment policy of an organisation, if one exists, will play a major part in how the candidates are selected. The policy may dictate if the position needs to be filled internally or externally, what type of questions must be asked in an interview and the affirmative action considerations for each candidate.

Number of applicants

The more candidates apply for the vacancy, the longer the process will take and the more complex it will be. It is a fine balance of having enough good candidates to choose from and having too many.

Information

The people responsible for selecting need as much information about the candidates as possible. The better informed they are, the better able they are to make the right decision.

Trade union pressure

The primary function of a trade union is to look after the well-being of its members. Trade unions will make sure the organisation abides by their recruitment policy and might put pressure on management to select and appoint its members.

External factors

External factors are those that cannot be controlled by an organisation. The external factors include the following:

Image of the organisation

The image of the organisation plays a critical role in the type and number of candidates applying for the vacant position. Potential candidates form their own perceptions – whether these are positive or negative – about the organisation, which are linked to the organisation's image. A positive image often creates the perception of better remuneration, promotion, recognition, good work environment, and so on, enhancing its reputation in the market, and thereby attracting the best possible resources.

Government requirements and regulations

The government statutory control is to protect both the employer and the employee, which will influence the selection process. The Employment Equity Act, No. 55 of 1998, in particular, will have an influence on the selection process.

Bribery

Bribery is also considered an external factor. Bribery is an act of offering a particular job to someone who is not the best candidate in exchange for money or some form of reward.

Nepotism (favouritism)

Nepotism is a form of discrimination in which family members or friends are hired although there might be a better qualified candidate applying for the position.

Competitors

Organisations in the same industry will compete for the best candidates to come and work for them.

Figure 2.5 As a human resource professional you cannot accept bribes or take part in unfair hiring practices.

Case study

Study the extracts from the news articles below:

Eskom's Matshela Koko tends his resignation

16 February 2018

Controversial Eskom executive, Matshela Koko, has now tended his resignation without admitting to any wrongdoing.

Private lenders insisted on Koko's dismissal before they would consider offering vital funding to the cash-strapped energy giant. Before Friday's hearing, Koko was adamant that he would not resign, saying he still had an important role to play at Eskom and that the lenders had been unfair in demanding his removal.

In January of 2018, Koko returned to Eskom after being acquitted in an earlier disciplinary hearing regarding allegations of nepotism involving his stepdaughter. The case against Koko claimed that he had helped his stepdaughter's company to score contracts worth R1 billion from Eskom.

to be continued...

Limpopo businessman busted for bribery

23 April 2018

Last Monday, a case was opened against a prominent Limpopo businessman who is suspected of offering bribes to government employees.

The businessman, who cannot be named yet, was found to have contravened multiple labour law regulations in his recruitment and placement practices in his company, Edge Cleaning Inc. He was found to be in contravention of the Labour Act, for which a compliance order was then issued.

According to the police spokesperson, instead of complying, the businessman allegedly approached the inspector from the department and promised to give him a R3000 bribe in order to forge the compliance report.

Criminal record or life sentence?

17 March 2017

"Even though I got my freedom back, it is almost impossible to find work. I think companies will never look at me the same way again. In interviews, everything goes well until they ask about my record." This is a statement made by an ex-convict who has been released and yet struggles to find employment.

This assumption is based on fact. According to Nicro (the National Institute for Crime Prevention and the Reintegration of Offenders), most South African employers disqualify applicants with a criminal record as a general recruitment policy without considering their applications on merit.

Figure 2.6 A criminal record can severely affect your future career options.

Questions:

1 Identify the factor that affects the screening and selection process in each of these articles. Give a reason for your answer.
2 Categorise these factors (from question 1) into either internal or external factors.

The screening and selection process

Screening and selection is a process of measurement, decision-making and evaluation. A well worked-out process will help to select the best candidate to fill the vacancy. The process guarantees consistency and helps to avoid unfair selection practices. The steps to follow are outlined below.

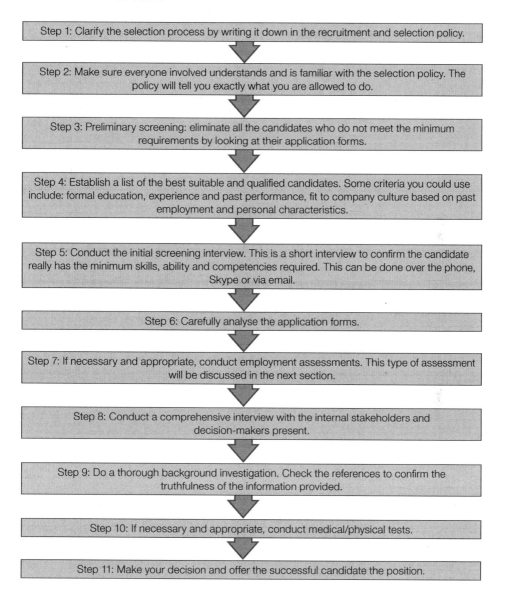

Step 1: Clarify the selection process by writing it down in the recruitment and selection policy.

Step 2: Make sure everyone involved understands and is familiar with the selection policy. The policy will tell you exactly what you are allowed to do.

Step 3: Preliminary screening: eliminate all the candidates who do not meet the minimum requirements by looking at their application forms.

Step 4: Establish a list of the best suitable and qualified candidates. Some criteria you could use include: formal education, experience and past performance, fit to company culture based on past employment and personal characteristics.

Step 5: Conduct the initial screening interview. This is a short interview to confirm the candidate really has the minimum skills, ability and competencies required. This can be done over the phone, Skype or via email.

Step 6: Carefully analyse the application forms.

Step 7: If necessary and appropriate, conduct employment assessments. This type of assessment will be discussed in the next section.

Step 8: Conduct a comprehensive interview with the internal stakeholders and decision-makers present.

Step 9: Do a thorough background investigation. Check the references to confirm the truthfulness of the information provided.

Step 10: If necessary and appropriate, conduct medical/physical tests.

Step 11: Make your decision and offer the successful candidate the position.

The selection process varies from organisation to organisation and even from department to department within the same organisation. In some organisations an initial interview and a comprehensive interview would be enough to make a final selection, while in others they may do an initial interview and then a second and third comprehensive interview before the final selection.

Screening as a cure for corruption

4 November 2016

Corruption is a huge problem in South Africa, and businesses are urged to tighten up their background screening processes in order to curb the tide of corrupt practices.

Ina van der Merwe, Director and CEO of Managed Integrity Evaluation (MIE), believes that if more isn't done to stop corruption in South Africa, this country could be considered the most corrupt in the world.

"Ongoing news stories paint a grim picture of the current state of fraud and corruption in South Africa, which, on the surface, seems to be on the increase. With this in mind, organisations need to start acting responsibly and invest in tools that can provide them with peace of mind.

"Whether organisations want to test the legitimacy of tenders, investigate corrupt links in their procurement chain, or vet potential job candidates, the onus is with organisations to reduce corruption."

For van der Merwe, screening candidates and vetting the procurement process within supply chains of organisations is of particular importance. "With the ongoing media coverage of high-profile individuals having been exposed for being dishonest about their qualifications and experience, it would be irresponsible for organisations not to implement stringent background screening measures.

"Realistically it is the only way to provide a level of certainty that the candidates they employ are who they say they are. Apart from the negative reputational and financial implications for organisations, proactive background screening also helps organisations to avoid increased recruitment costs.

"Conducting comprehensive background screening advances companies' HR and risk and compliance strategies, which in turn will have a direct effect on reducing corruption in the long run. This would result in an increase in public confidence, shifting the perception that South Africa is the most corrupt country."

Screening strategies

An organisation may use different strategies to assess potential candidates as part of the screening process. They invest an enormous amount of money, time and other resources in advertising and recruiting strategies to attract the best candidates and want to eliminate candidates who are not suitable as early as possible. Screening strategies usually include some kind of preliminary test to see if the candidate is appropriate.

Psychometric testing

There are a number different types of tests that a human resources department might deem necessary for a particular role. The industry of the organisation will often determine the type of screening tests the potential candidate will need to do. Some of the screening tests companies may use have been listed below.

Motor skills competency test

This is generally used in industries that require manual labour or physical skills, for example, a bricklayer or machinist may have to do a test of their particular abilities before being considered for the role.

Aptitude test

This test is normally conducted if you want to find out what someone is naturally good at and to determine if they have the ability to do a particular task. It can be used for jobs such as designers or engineers.

Cognitive ability test

This is the IQ (intelligence quotient) test most of us are familiar with. Some organisations still use an IQ test as part of their screening and selection process. Testing is legal as long as a professionally-developed employment test is administered according to the test developer's intended use. Additionally, it's the application of the test that makes the difference between whether issuing an IQ test is "legal" or "illegal". For example, it's perfectly legal to give accounting applicants a mathematics test. However, it could be considered a discriminatory practice to screen a prison warden using the same mathematics test, because mathematical competency is not necessary for a prison warden.

Interest test

Interest tests help you define your interests and determine what you like most. The main reason for an interest test is to match your interests with a career that you would be suited to and enjoy doing. It is a series of questions of what you like or dislike. The key is to match these preferences with a career.

If you enjoy something and it matches your interests, you are more likely to be successful, efficient and effective in your job.

Personality test

Personality tests can be used in the early part of the screening and selection process to identify people who have the right personality attributes to fit into a particular role or team within an organisation. These tests identify far more than just the knowledge and skills for a particular job.

Some companies put teams together according to their personalities. Organisations might also like to know what kind of people they are dealing with in order for managers to know how to get the best out of people. Personality tests are often conducted in bigger corporations. The Myers-Briggs test and the Enneagram are examples of personality tests.

Assessment centres

Some organisations use assessment centres to help them with candidate selection. These centres assess certain competencies through simulation exercises. They create a real-life situation to see if the candidate is able to do the job. Assessment centres offer very good and reliable ways of assessing certain required skills and behaviours. Unfortunately these centres are usually expensive and the assessments are time consuming.

Validity and reliability of the assessments

- **Validity** is the extent to which a test accurately measures what it is supposed to measure.
- **Reliability** is the degree to which the assessment tool produces stable and consistent results.

Did you know? The Health Professions Council of South Africa has a list of psychological tests that include the approved workplace testing that can be conducted. You can view the list here: http://www.hpcsa.co.za

Techniques for conducting interviews

Almost all organisations use interviews as a selection mechanism. The interview is a vital part of the recruitment process as it is the most popular tool in making a selection decision.

An interview is normally a face-to-face conversation between the interviewer (the person conducting the interview) and the interviewee (the person being interviewed), although sometimes interviews are conducted over the phone or using video conferencing technology, such as Skype. This gives candidates who are geographically separated from the employer the opportunity to be interviewed.

Interviews generally last 30–45 minutes, depending on the level of appointment. More senior positions might require interviews that last longer than an hour. Also, a preliminary screening interview may be shorter than a more in-depth second interview when a small number of candidates are in the running for the same position.

Just as is the case with tests for different industries, there are also different types of interviews depending on what kind of job is being interviewed for. Generally, an organisation will have more than one set of interviews.

Interviews can be classified by their degree of structure, or the extent to which the interviewer plans the questions in advance and asks the same questions of all the candidates for the job. We will be looking at the following types of interviews:

- Structured interviews
- Unstructured interviews
- Semi-structured interviews
- Panel interviews
- Stress interviews.

> **DEFINITIONS**
>
> **validity** – the extent to which the assessment tool accurately measures what it is supposed to measure
>
> **reliability** – the degree to which the assessment tool produces stable and consistent results

Structured interviews

Structured interviews are the most reliable form of interview. The questions for the candidates are pre-planned and each candidate is asked the same set of questions. Most of the questions are closed-ended which do not give the interviewee the opportunity to elaborate on their answers.

Below are some examples of closed-ended questions that may be asked in a structured interview:
- When can you start?
- Are you willing to relocate?
- Would you be comfortable with 50% travel?
- Where did you go to college?

The **advantage** of a structured interview is:
- Information is gathered in a uniform manner. This makes the interview fair, consistent and valid.

The **disadvantage** of a structured interview is:
- The information might be very limited because of the closed-ended questions.

Unstructured interviews

Unstructured interviews are just the opposite of structured interviews. No question is pre-planned. The questions are open-ended, which means the candidate may elaborate on their answers. This type of interview can only be conducted by an experienced interviewer.

Here are some examples of open-ended questions and answers:

Q: How do you evaluate success?
   A: "For me, success is about doing my job well. I want to be recognised as someone who always tries their hardest to reach their goals."
Q: Why are you leaving your job?
   A: "I've decided that my current work role is not the direction I want to go in my career and my current employer has no opportunities in the direction I am heading."

The **advantage** of an unstructured interview is:
- The candidate has the opportunity to elaborate on their answers. They can give more detailed answers and feedback.

Some **disadvantages** of an unstructured interview are:
- The information gathered is non-conclusive about how well they performed in the workplace.
- The interviewer might be biased towards a specific interviewee.
- To compare the candidates will also be difficult because the questions will not be the same.

Semi-structured interviews

Semi-structured interviews can be seen as a combination of the previous two techniques. The most important questions are pre-planned and asked of all the candidates. This technique also gives the opportunity for the interviewer to ask any other question(s) that may come up as the interview develops.

The **advantage** of a semi-structured interview is:
- The interviewer will not only be able to get specific information, but also to get some idea of the candidate's personality, values and beliefs.

A **disadvantage** of this type of interview is:
- It can be time consuming and can only be conducted by experienced interviewers.

Structured interviews may be used in an initial screening interview, when the number of candidates is quite large. Unstructured interviews review personal details of the candidate, so as to judge if he/she is the right person for the job. This may be used in a second or third round of interviews. The semi-structured interview is the most frequently used technique, especially if the organisation is only going to do one interview and wants to combine different types of questions. The decision of which interview to use will vary depending on the organisation and circumstances.

Panel interviews

A panel interview aims to analyse the candidate's skill set and the candidate's overall efficiency in handling a team of members with multiple questions. The panel is usually made up of three to five people. Each member on the panel is a specialist in their field and will ask a question that is related to that particular field. Each panel member will also have some dealings with the new candidate once they have been selected for their role. Often, representatives of a particular team will be invited to interview new team members who they may work closely with. One person will lead the panel and make sure the interview flows without unnecessary delays between interviewers.

Figure 2.7 A panel interview

The interviewers will usually meet beforehand to prepare for the interview.

Because of the complexity of the role in your organisation, a panel interview places a candidate under greater scrutiny, resulting in a more carefully evaluated hire and one who can thrive under pressure.

Panel interviews are most common in the following fields and positions, although you may find them in other employment sectors as well, such as:

- Academic institutions
- Large non-profit organisations
- Senior executive positions across many industries
- Government organisations and related agencies.

The **advantages** of a panel interview are:

- Instead of conducting many rounds of interviews with different interviewers, you will save time by gathering them all on a panel.
- The different perspectives from the specialists will help to gain a better assessment and candidate choice.

A **disadvantage** of a panel interview is:

- It can be time consuming, as each member of the panel needs to prepare beforehand and assemble at a single venue.

Figure 2.8 A panel interview incorporates different perspectives to assess candidates better.

Stress interviews

Some industries involve working in high-stress environments, like journalists, project managers or security guards. These kinds of roles require a person to remain calm and collected under pressure. This interview intentionally wants to see if the candidate will be able to handle this stressful environment.

The interviewer wants to put the candidate in a simulated situation to that of the work environment to see how the candidate performs.

The interviewer may use:

Intimidating questions

"Why were you fired from your last job?" "Was your previous job too much for you to handle?" These aggressive questions are intended to put you on the spot.

Aggressive behaviour

This is hostile behaviour towards the candidate to see how he/she responds, to see if the candidate can keep their "cool" in an emotional situation. Aggressive behaviour can include behaviours like swearing, shouting, using sarcasm, facial expressions and threatening gestures.

Unexpected responses

The interviewer may ask the same question multiple times, pretending that he/she forgot or did not comprehend your answer as you grow more frustrated at their lack of understanding.

Brainteasers

"How many rats are there in Johannesburg?" While you're not expected to know off the top of your head, you need to demonstrate your ability to explain how you would research the answer, and how you can stay calm and think logically.

An **advantage** of a stress interview is:
* The interviewer will quickly see if the candidate can handle stress and will gain useful insight into how they react.

The **disadvantages** of a stress interview are:
* It can be a time consuming interview.
* It can only conducted by experienced interviewers.
* The candidate may get an unrealistically negative impression of the interviewer if the interviewer is hostile towards them, which may affect their willingness to work for this company.

Example 1

Stress interview questions
* What has been the most embarrassing moment in your entire life?
* How do you feel about working for twenty hours at a stretch?
* What is the worst thing that you have heard about our company?
* Do you have any enemies at your previous workplace?
* How would you evaluate me as an interviewer?

Evaluation of the screening and selection process

Employing the right people for your business is of the utmost importance. The organisation has to evaluate and determine if they made the correct appointment and that the process was cost effective.

There are certain factors directly related to the success of the selection process:
* Increased productivity and quality
* Reduced turnover and absenteeism
* Reduced risk of legal challenges
* Reduced risk of aberrant (abnormal or unacceptable) behaviours
* Improved resource utilisation.

If the factors mentioned above are not in place or the opposite happens, that is a clear indication that there is a problem with the recruitment process.

In Module 3 we will study the evaluation of an employee's performance, staff turnover and absenteeism.

Figure 2.9 Selecting the right people to fill a position is essential for the effective running of an organisation.

UNIT 2.3 **Affirmative action**

What is affirmative action?

Affirmative action in South Africa is defined in the Employment Equity Act, No. 55 of 1998, ("the Act") as:

"Measures designed to ensure that suitably qualified people from designated groups have equal employment opportunities and are equitably represented in all occupational categories and levels in the workforce of a designated employer."

In the past, black people (which includes black, coloured and Indian people), women and people with disabilities were underrepresented in many areas of the work force. This has resulted in an unequal distribution of these previously disadvantaged people in positions of top management to this day.

The Employment Equity Act, No. 55 of 1998, and the Employment Equity Amended Act, No. 47 of 2013, aim to redress fundamental labour market inequities. South Africa's Constitution aims to ensure equal opportunities for all. By doing this, the Constitution ensures that the discriminatory approach and practices of the past are not continued or repeated in the future.

No person or organisation may unfairly discriminate, directly or indirectly, against an employee on the basis of race, gender, age, disability, HIV status, sexual orientation, language, pregnancy, political opinion and religious beliefs, amongst other things.

The Employment Equity Act, No. 55 of 1998, applies to all employers, workers and even job applicants, but not members of the National Defence Force, National Intelligence Agency and South African Secret Service.

Affirmative action versus employment equity

Affirmative action is what springs to mind for many when employment equity is mentioned.

Many business owners and managers use the terms "affirmative action" and "employment equity" interchangeably. Both have the purpose of ensuring that the workplace is non-discriminatory and representative of the population, but there are significant differences between the two.

Affirmative action is the short term labour policy aimed at redressing the inequalities of the past and, in so doing, achieving a transformed workplace, which is representative of the greater South Africa. The Department of Labour defines affirmative action as the process of ensuring that qualified people from designated groups have equal opportunities in the workplace.

Employment equity takes the long term view. Affirmative action falls under the Employment Equity Act, No. 55 of 1998, which provides a framework for implementing affirmative action. Employment equity ensures that the past situation never repeats itself and that all South Africans have equal access to employment opportunities and to advancement within the workplace.

Employment equity is the link between affirmative action (number crunching), equal opportunity (levelling the playing fields), and managing diversity (celebrating our differences). Affirmative action is a strategy within the employment equity framework with the specific purpose of addressing the wrongs of the past and putting them right.

Formulation and implementation of affirmative action

A designated employer must implement affirmative action for designated groups. Designated employers are employers who employ 50 or more people, or have an annual turnover of more than the amount specified in Schedule 4 of the Employment Equity Act (see Figure 2.11 below).

Designated groups are black people (including black, coloured and Indian people), women and people with disabilities. Designated groups must be represented as they are represented by the population in all job categories and all levels of the workplace, including the top levels of management. For example, if you have 50 members on your board of directors, then you must aim to have approximately 35 black, five coloured, four Indian and five white directors. Of these, 25 should be female and two should be disabled.

Designated employers should have an action plan, such as an employment equity plan, which sets out how they are to achieve workplace diversity.

According to the Department of Labour, the employment equity plan should include the following (based on Section 20 of the Employment Equity Act, No. 55 of 1998):

1. The objectives for every year
2. Affirmative action measures that will be implemented
3. Where a designated group is not represented:
   - numerical goals to reach this
   - timetables
   - strategies
4. Timetables for annual objectives
5. The duration of the plan (minimum a year and maximum 5 years)
6. Procedures that will be used to monitor and evaluate the implementation of the plan
7. Ways to solve disputes about the plan
8. The people responsible for implementing the plan.

Employment Equity Act

Schedule 4

Annual Turnover Threshold – Revised January 2014

Industrial Sector	OLD Total Annual Turnover	NEW Total Annual Turnover
Agriculture	R 2,00m	R 6,00m
Mining and Quarrying	R 7,50m	R 22,50m
Manufacturing	R10,00m	R30,00m
Electricity, Gas and Water	R10,00m	R30,00m
Construction	R 5,00m	R 15,00m
Retail and Motor Trade and Repair Services	R15,00m	R45,00m
Wholesale Trade, Commercial Agents and Allied Services	R25,00m	R75,00m
Catering, Accommodation and Other Trade	R 5,00m	R 15,00m
Transport, Storage and Communications	R10,00m	R30,00m
Finance and Business Services	R10,00m	R30,00m
Community, Social and Personal Services	R 5,00m	R 15,00m

Figure 2.10 The annual turnover of a designated employer

Skills development has been a high priority of the government for many years. However, factors such as the lack of space at tertiary level and a lack of funding have forced the government to consider other opportunities to upskill the nation. The Black Economic Empowerment (BEE) programme (2003) was introduced to increase opportunities for previously disadvantaged individuals. Since then, the government modified the programme; called Broad-Based Black Economic Empowerment (BBBEE) in 2007, with more updates and modifications to improve the programme in 2013 and 2015.

Companies urged to review employment equity plans

16 August 2017
Cape Town

The Department of Labour is strengthening its attempts to root out JSE listed companies that contravene the Employment Equity (EE) Act, and amendments made recently will see businesses facing even harsher penalties for non-compliance.

The act was issued in 1998 to be applied by all employers who employ more than 50 members of staff or have an annual turnover above a certain threshold.

These companies must create and implement an employment equity plan in order to "redress disparities in employment", eliminating unfair discrimination and promoting the right to equality.

Entities and organisations employing over 150 employees are required to issue their EE plan to the department on the first working day in October every year. Employers with fewer than 150 employees need to submit their plan biennially.

In addition, public entities are required to include a summary of their plan in their annual financial reports. The department of labour supplied a table that must be included in this report, summarising the occupational levels of the employees together with the statistics highlighting their nationalities and gender.

At the time of its latest announcement, the SA Revenue Service (SARS) had stated its intention to look at all employment equity reports. Where these were not correct or not in compliance, they would impose fines.

"Clearly this has not been correctly applied over the years. The Department of Labour has singled out the JSE Limited as one of the offenders warned to get their house in order," said a spokesperson.

"The latest decision taken by the Department of Labour was that if a company does not have a plan, it will be issued a fine of R1.5 million. Additionally, those failing to report on EE plans will also be subjected to a penalty of R1.5m," said a spokesperson.

"Companies that did report an EE plan, but do not actually have or apply it will possibly even be taken to criminal courts. Labour Minister Mildred Oliphant also warned that the department would proclaim section 53 of the EE Act to block non-compliant companies from doing business with the state."

Figure 2.11 Companies without an employment equity plan could be fined up to R1.5 million.

to be continued...

Questions

Use the information that you have learned so far and the news article to answer the
questions below.

1 What is the purpose of the Employment Equity Act, No. 55 of 1998?
2 How will it help workers and managers?
3 What are some examples of unfair discrimination that the law prevents?
4 Who is responsible for developing the employment equity plan?
5 Who are designated employers?
6 Explain the concept of designated groups.

Did you know? You can visit the Department of Labour's website to read about
affirmative action and employment equity: www.labour.gov.za

UNIT 2.4 **Placement**

Once an organisation establishes a candidate's unique profile and selects the specific
individual, this employee must be placed in their job. **Placement** is a process of assigning
a specific job to a selected candidate. It involves assigning a specific rank and
responsibility to an individual. It also involves matching the requirements of a job with the
qualifications of the candidate. Placement can be seen as the starting point of career
management.

"Did you place an advert for an experienced sitter?"

Figure 2.12 Job placement involves finding a candidate suited to
the role.

DEFINITION

placement – the process of assigning a specific job to a selected candidate

The aim of placement in the work environment

This section will answer the question of why placement in the work environment is necessary. An individual is selected for their specific skills, abilities, qualifications and experience, which can help the organisation to reach its goals. Thus the organisation wants to utilise these skills as soon as possible for its own benefit.

If the candidate is selected for a role, adjusts well to the job and continues to perform per expectations, it means that the candidate is properly placed. However, if the candidate is seen to have problems adjusting to the job, the human resources department must find out whether the person is properly placed.

Proper placement of employees will lower the chances of employee absenteeism, staff turnover, accidents, etc. It is also beneficial to the candidate to be properly placed. The candidate will be more satisfied and contented with their work if they have the appropriate skills and abilities to excel in their role.

Placement strategies

To make sure a candidate's abilities and the job requirements match, the organisation can use the following strategies:

Internal labour market strategy
According to this strategy, all new appointments of people from outside the organisation are made to entry-level posts only. Current workers who possess the potential are appointed (promoted and transferred) to higher-level positions.

The advantage of this strategy is that current employees are already part of the organisation. It promotes enterprise loyalty and commitment. The disadvantage of internal labour market strategy is that a new employee who possesses the ability and qualifications to perform the job at a more advanced level must start at an entry-level post.

External labour market strategy
The external labour market strategy appoints new employees to any level of the organisational hierarchy. No provision is made for promotions. This recruitment function needs to be well-managed, because high staff turnover may be a result of a lack of promotions. This is usually a good strategy for a business with a flat organisational structure, specifically in areas such as the scientific and medical professions.

Experimental placing
It is not always possible to make a perfect match between what a job requires and what the candidate can offer. For this reason an organisation may place the candidate in a temporary position. If the organisation is certain the candidate is able to perform the required tasks to the approved standard, and the employee is happy with their reward and work environment, the position will be made permanent. This is a "try it before you buy it" approach.

Labour pool placing
This is a strategy for potential employees to get used to the working environment. They are appointed in a temporary capacity until such time as a permanent position becomes vacant. The advantage of the labour pool strategy is that the organisation uses the labour

pool to fill in for permanent staff who are sick, on leave or have resigned. The disadvantage is that it is costly to maintain a pool of temporary staff.

Interim placement

Sometimes the margin is very small between the candidate selected for the position and the next candidate in line (the second choice). Organisations do not want to lose that candidate, so they might employ them in a temporary position while they decide where best they can utilise them.

Another use of interim placement is where a candidate is appointed to a position before it actually falls vacant. For example, when someone is about to retire you want the transition to go smoothly, so you might employ someone as an understudy to the outgoing employee.

Placement implementation

There are several methods of implementing placement:

Promotion

Promotion is the upward movement in the organisational structure, for example, from an assistant manager to a manager position. This upward movement is usually accompanied by more responsibility, greater authority, a higher salary and higher status.

Transfers

A transfer is the horizontal movement between departments or branches (job families). The level of the position, responsibility, authority, salary and status remain the same. For example, a bank teller at Absa Cape Town can be transferred to the same position at another branch, like Absa Stellenbosch.

Demotion

Demotion involves the movement to a lower position in the organisation's structure. The level of responsibility, authority, salary and status will also be decreased. Demotion is the result of poor job performance over time or of the worker's gross negligence. Organisations sometimes use demotion as a form of disciplinary action, although it is not seen as an official disciplinary sanction.

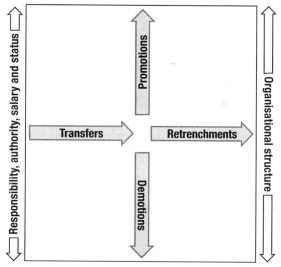

Figure 2.13 Placement methods

Retrenchments

Retrenchment is the reduction in the number of employees in the organisation. This usually happens as a result of financial considerations. Most of the time, it is a short term strategy in difficult financial times and poor economic conditions. As soon as the situation changes for the better–the organisation is in a better financial position and the demand is high for the organisation's products–the retrenched workers are the first to be re-employed.

UNIT 2.5 **Induction**

Now that the right candidate has been selected and placed within the organisation, the process of induction begins. The successful candidate receives a letter of appointment welcoming them and asking them to report to work on a specific day. The letter of appointment is the official starting point of induction. This is the first step towards gaining an employee's commitment.

Induction refers to the process of welcoming and receiving the new employee to the organisation, and preparing them for their new role. The employee will be introduced to the organisation's culture, history, traditions, departments, people, policies, procedures and to the specific work he/she will do.

Figure 2.14 Induction is an important part of your first few days at a new job.

The aim of induction

A new worker is faced with a new environment, new people, new job, new equipment and, in many cases, a new location. All these changes cause uncertainty and for this reason a proper induction process is of the utmost importance.

The aim of induction is:
- To make the first days where everything is unfamiliar much easier. First impressions last, and therefore the employee's impressions should be good ones.
- To familiarise the new employee with the requirements of the job
- To explain the terms and conditions to the employee
- To provide information to the employee regarding the organisation's policies and procedures
- To instil a positive attitude regarding the organisation, and towards the organisation's policies and procedures
- To improve the employee's morale
- To make the new employee productive more quickly
- To improve the quality of production and service delivery

- To increase the level of job satisfaction experienced by the employee
- To lower the chances of employee's absenteeism and staff turnover
- To prevent accidents and wastage of materials
- To create realistic expectations and goals.

The induction programme

The specific details of an induction programme, such as length and content, will vary across organisations and according to the level of the position. Smaller organisations' induction programmes might be more informal and larger organisations' more formal. Induction programmes should develop theoretical and practical skills, but also meet interaction needs that exist among the new employees.

An induction programme can include the following:
- The organisation's history, core values, mission and vision
- The organisation's products/services
- The departments' locations
- Personnel policies and procedures
- Terms and conditions of services, like hours, leave, medical leave, etc. will have
- Grievance, retrenchment and disciplinary procedures
- Remuneration and other fringe benefits
- Health and safety measures.

Induction is part of socialisation. Socialisation is the process of adaptation, where a new employee goes through different phases while they adapt to the new work environment. The three phases of induction are outlined below:

Pre-arrival

This is your first encounter with the organisation. It starts with how you are treated in your interview, the communication thereafter and your acceptance of the offer of employment. This includes the phone call, the appointment letter and your contract of employment. You, as a new employee, already formed some perception of the organisation. It is the organisation's responsibility to create a positive perception. It is a good idea to appoint a mentor to meet and guide the new employee once he or she arrives.

Encounter

In this stage, the employee will go through the general induction programme (also known to many as the general orientation programme). This will serve as an introduction to the organisation's history, core values, mission and vision; the organisation's products and services; the departments' locations; personnel policies and procedures; terms and conditions of services, etc. This stage's goal is to instil a positive attitude in the employee and to make the new employee productive as soon as possible.

Metamorphosis

This is the stage where an employee is no longer seen as a new employee. The employee went through a metamorphosis (change) and now sees themself as one of the staff. It is now "us" and not "I" and "them". The employee adapts to the new work culture, builds confidence and is able to sort out problems they may encounter in the work environment on their own.

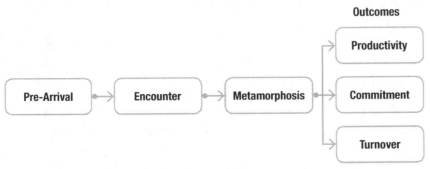

Figure 2.15 The socialisation model of induction

The evaluation of the induction programme

The organisation wants the new employee to perform as soon as possible to an expected standard. To this end, it is important to evaluate the induction programme to make sure that it is meeting these standards. Proper induction would enable the employee to get off to a good start and to develop their overall effectiveness on the job and enhance their potential.

While the human resources staff will normally provide general orientation relating to the organisation, the immediate supervisor should take the responsibility for specific orientation relating to the job and fellow employees can also assist their new colleague.

The follow-up of orientation is to be co-ordinated by both the human resources department and the supervisor with a view mainly to obtain feedback and provide guidance and counselling as required.

Example 2

New employees might be asked to complete an evaluation, like the one below, when their induction complete.

Please complete the following evaluation form and return it the human resources manager. Thank you for your time.

1 Please rate the overall quality of the induction program

☐ Exceptional ☐ Very good ☐ Good ☐ Average ☐ Needs improvement

2 How well did the induction programme prepare you for your new role?

☐ Exceptional ☐ Very good ☐ Good ☐ Average ☐ Needs improvement

3 How well did the induction brief you on the organisation's vision, strategies, culture, policies and procedures?

☐ Exceptional ☐ Very good ☐ Good ☐ Average ☐ Needs improvement

4 How effective was the induction programme in introducing you to your colleagues, systems and processes of the organisation?

☐ Exceptional ☐ Very good ☐ Good ☐ Average ☐ Needs improvement

WHAT DO WE KNOW AND WHERE TO NEXT...

Revisiting the learning objectives

Now that you have completed this module you should have achieved the learning objectives listed in the table below:

Learning objective	What you have learned	Tick box
Explain briefly what is meant by recruitment in work practice.	Definition of **recruitment**: Searching for and placing candidates in open positions within an organisation.	☐
Describe in a pragmatic way the importance of a recruitment policy.	The recruitment policy is a document that stipulates detailed guidelines on how an organisation deals with recruitment.	☐
Indicate which factors influence recruitment in an organisation in the South African context.	**External factors:** • The economy and labour market conditions • Supply and demand • Political and legal consideration • Affirmative action • Trade unions • The technological environment • The image of the organisation. **Internal factors:** • The recruiting policy of the organisation • The cost of recruitment • The organisational culture • The recruitment standards • The size of the organisation.	☐ ☐
Identify internal and external sources of recruitment and the practical implications thereof.	**External sources:** • Advertisement – direct applications • E-recruitment • Private employment agencies • Public employment agencies • Campus recruitment • Recommendations/referrals • Head hunters • Walk-ins • Temporary employees. **Internal sources:** • Promotion • Transfer • Word of mouth • Internal employee referral/recommendation • Internal advertising (present database) • Notice boards.	☐ ☐

Learning objective	What you have learned	Tick box
Use recruitment processes as applicable in the South African work environment.	**The recruitment process:** Step 1: Identify the vacancy and evaluate the organisation's need Step 2: Develop a job description Step 3: Develop a recruitment plan Step 4: Selected committee makes plans on how and when to advertise the vacancy Step 5: Post the vacancy and implement the recruitment plan Step 6: Review résumés and short list the best applications Step 7: Candidates are invited for interviews and selection tests Step 8: Conduct face-to-face interview Step 9: Prepare for the selection process.	☐
Discuss how and why the recruitment process of an organisation is evaluated for effectiveness in practice.	It is important to evaluate the organisation's recruitment process according to the following: quality, speed, and cost.	☐
Explain briefly what is meant by screening and selection in the personnel recruitment practice.	**Screening:** the organisation evaluates applicants' qualifications. Candidates who do not meet the minimum requirements needed for the position are eliminated. The objective is to identify the most qualified candidates for the vacant position. **Selection:** the next process of measurement, decision-making and evaluation. This is a process of putting the right candidate in the right job. It is a procedure of matching organisational requirements with the skills and qualifications of the potential candidate.	☐
Identify which factors of the internal and external environment affect the screening of candidates.	**Internal factors:** • Size of organisation • Recruiting policy • Image of the organisation • Number of applicants • Information • Trade union pressure. **External factors:** • Government requirements and regulations • Bribery • Nepotism (favouritism).	☐

Learning objective	What you have learned	Tick box
Demonstrate the steps in the screening process in a pragmatic way.	**Screening process:** Step 1: Clarify the selection process. Step 2: Make sure everyone involved understands and is familiar with the selection policy. The policy will tell you exactly what to and what you allowed to do. Step 3: Do the preliminary screening. Eliminate all the candidates who do not meet the minimum requirements. Step 4: Establish a list of finalists. Step 5: Conduct the initial screening interview. This is a short interview to confirm the candidate really has the minimum skills, ability and competencies required. Step 6: Analysing the application forms. Step 7: If necessary and appropriate, conduct employment assessments. Step 8: Conduct a comprehensive interview. Step 9: Do a thorough background investigation. Check the references to confirm the truthfulness of the information provided. Step 10: If necessary and appropriate, conduct medical/physical tests. Step 11: Make your decision and offer the successful candidate the position.	☐
Differentiate between different screening techniques.	**Screening strategies:** • Motor skills competency test • Aptitude test • Cognitive ability test • Interest test • Personality test • Assessment centres.	☐
Demonstrate how to conduct interviews in the screening process to ensure effective selection in practice.	Techniques for **conducting interviews:** • Structured interviews • Unstructured interviews • Semi-structured interviews • Panel interviews • Stress interviews.	☐
Describe the measures used to evaluate the screening and selection process.	The organisation has to evaluate and determine if they made the correct appointment and that the process was cost effective and will lead to: • Increased productivity and quality • Reduced turnover and absenteeism • Reduced risk of legal challenges • Reduced risk of aberrant (abnormal and unacceptable) behaviours • Improved resource utilisation.	☐

Learning objective	What you have learned	Tick box
Describe the meaning of affirmative action as a strategy in the recruitment process and the practical implications thereof.	• **Affirmative action** is a short term labour policy • It is aimed at redressing the inequalities of the past and achieving a transformed workplace, which is representative of South Africa. • Affirmative action falls under the Employment Equity Act, No. 55 of 1998, which provides a framework for implementing affirmative action. • Employment equity is a long term policy. • Employment equity ensures that the past situation never repeats itself and that all South Africans have equal access to employment opportunities and advancement within the workplace.	☐
Discuss affirmative action as a means of employee development in the South African work environment.	• Designated employers are employers who employ 50 or more people, or who have an annual turnover of more than the amount specified in Schedule 4 of the Employment Equity Act, No. 55 of 1998,. • Designated groups are black people, women and people with disabilities. Designated groups must be equally represented in all jobs categories and levels of the workplace. • Skills development via tertiary education has obstacles, e.g. a lack of space and funding, so the government had to consider other opportunities to upskill the nation. • The Black Economic Empowerment (BEE) programme (2003) was introduced to increase opportunities for previously disadvantaged individuals.	☐
Explain briefly the formulation and implementation of affirmative action in practice.	**Formulating an employment equity plan** includes: • Analysing the demographic profile of the organisation's current workforce • A manager who is responsible for handling employment equity issues • Find and remove barriers/issues that badly affect designated groups • Preparing the employment equity plan • Reporting on workforce diversity to the Department of Labour • Ensuring equal representation of designated groups in all jobs categories and levels of the workplace • Retain and develop designated groups.	☐
Explain briefly what is meant by placement as part of personnel recruitment practice.	Placement is the process of assigning a specific job to a selected candidate. It involves assigning a specific rank and responsibility to an individual.	☐
Describe the aim of placement in the work environment.	An individual is selected for their specific skills, abilities, qualifications and experience which can help the organisation to reach its goals. Thus the organisation wants to utilise these skills as soon as possible for its own benefit.	☐

Learning objective	What you have learned	Tick box
Differentiate between different placement strategies in practice.	**Placement strategies:** • Internal labour market strategy • External labour market strategy • Experimental placing • Labour pool placing • Interim placement.	☐
Explain the different methods or techniques for placement which are currently applied in the work environment.	**Implementation of placement strategies:** • Promotion • Transfers • Demotion • Retrenchments	☐
• Explain what is meant by induction.	Induction refers to the process of welcoming and receiving the new employee to the organisation.	☐
Discuss the aim of effective induction in the work environment.	**Aim of induction:** • To make the first days easier and smoother • To familiarise the new employee with the requirements of the job • To explain the terms and conditions to the employee • To provide information to the employee regarding the organisation's policies and procedures • To install a positive attitude regarding the organisation, and to the organisation's policies and procedures • To improve the employee's morale • To make the new employee productive more quickly • To improve the quality of production and service delivery • To increase the level of job satisfaction experienced by the employee • To lower the chances of employee's absenteeism and staff turnover • To prevent accidents and wastage of materials • To create realistic expectations and goals.	☐
Explain in a pragmatic way the different components of an induction programme, including general orientation of the new employee.	An **induction programme** includes the following: • The organisation's history, core values, mission and vision • The organisation's products/services • The departments' locations • Personnel policies and procedures • Terms and conditions of services, like hours, leave, medical leave, etc. • Grievance, retrenchment and disciplinary procedures • Remuneration and other fringe benefits • Health and safety measures.	☐
	It is very important to evaluate the organisation's induction process. Proper induction would enable the employee to get off to a good start and to develop their overall effectiveness on the job and enhance their potential.	☐

Assessment

True or false

Choose whether the following statements are TRUE or FALSE. Write only the number of the question followed by 'true' or 'false'.

1. Recruitment is the timely and cost effective search for a candidate whose competencies match the skills of the vacancy.
2. The benefits of recruitment from within the organisation are cost-saving and increased motivation.
3. A measure of employment equity is to promote diversity and to accommodate people from all groups.
4. Promotions, employment, induction, transfers and demotions are examples of placement strategies.
5. Parties responsible for the induction process are, amongst others, the human resources department and the immediate manager.

(5 × 2) [10]

Multiple choice questions

Choose the correct answer from the various options provided. Choose only A, B, C or D and write your answer next to the question number.

1. Which of the following is not an example of internal recruitment resources? (2)
   - A Promotions
   - B Campus recruitment
   - C Transfers
   - D Word of mouth

2. Identify the example of a specific cognitive ability. (2)
   - A Reasoning
   - B Clarity
   - C Conduct
   - D Education

3. No person may discriminate against another human being. Which of the following is not discrimination? (2)
   - A Age
   - B Gender
   - C HIV status
   - D Dismissal

4. In this stage the goal is to instil a positive attitude in the employee. (2)
   - A Pre-arrival
   - B Encounter
   - C Metamorphosis
   - D Introduction

5. As soon as the situation changes for the better, these workers are the first to be employed. (2)
    A   Transferred
    B   Promoted
    C   Demoted
    D   Retrenched

                                                                    (5 × 2) [10]

Short questions

Briefly answer the following questions:

1. Explain walk-ins as an external recruitment source. (4)
2. Explain the terms validity and reliability of testing. (3 × 2)
3. Define the following terms/concepts:
    a) Selection (2)
    b) Head hunters (2)
    c) Screening. (2)
4. Name any FOUR methods of placement. (4)

                                                                        [20]

Long questions

Answer the following questions as comprehensively as you can:

1. Discuss the following methods of interviewing applicants:
    a) Structured interviews (9)
    b) Stress interviews (9)
    c) Panel interviews. (9)
2. Name EIGHT factors influencing the selection process. (8)
3. Some organisations prefer to promote their present employees rather than recruiting from outside the company. Indicate why this decision could be to the advantage of the organisation. (5 × 2)
4. Explain why it is important for a new employee to attend the induction programme. (10)
5. What is the aim of the recruitment policy? (5)

                                                                        [60]
                                                        Grand total: 100 marks

COMPENSATION MANAGEMENT

This module covers the following:

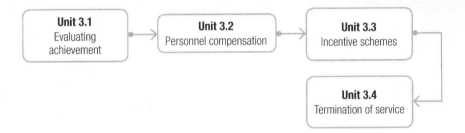

Learning objectives

By the end of this module, you should be able to do the following:
- Differentiate between terms regarding employee achievement such as performance appraisal, personnel ratings, rating scales and work standards
- Explain the use of achievement awards in practice
- Describe potential problems related to performance appraisal which may prevent its effectiveness in practice
- Differentiate between different achievement evaluation techniques and methods used in practice in South Africa
- Define basic terms regarding remuneration, such as nett wages, take-home pay, salaries, commission, bonuses and fringe benefits
- Explain the reason for the importance of personnel compensation in the work environment
- Explain the basic processes in wage and salary administration in a pragmatic way
- Describe the different components of a personnel compensation system
- Compile a compensation package according to principles used in South African labour practice
- Discuss the nature and purpose of job evaluation in practice
- Describe the different job evaluation system briefly
- Explain how job evaluation data is used to develop the pay structure of an organisation

- Differentiate between different kinds of incentive schemes used in practice in addition to the basic wage structure
- Indicate the purpose and advantages of incentive schemes in the effective management of a compensation policy in practice
- Discuss the procedures to be followed in the case of the termination of service of an employee and the problems which are experienced in this regard.

Key terms

achievement	feedback	nett pay (take-home pay)
bonus	fringe benefits	performance appraisal
commission	gross pay	performance management
dismissal	incentive	termination of service

Starting point

Julian and the organisation's management are happy with the latest appointments and transfers that have taken place. All staff members are settled in their positions and know what is expected of them. The president wants to make sure the organisation maintains its current personnel and everyone is performing to their full potential.

Julian is busy planning for the appraisal process that will take place in the next few weeks. This will be an excellent opportunity to find out how everyone is performing. He also needs to determine if everyone is rewarded fairly and who is entitled to a bonus. There was also a request from the trade union to add an incentive scheme and medical aid as a benefit to next year's remuneration budget.

Julian knows that the performance tools and techniques the organisation currently uses will provide him and his department with all the necessary information.

Figure 3.1 Julian's manager meets with one of the employees for an appraisal

UNIT 3.1 Evaluating achievement

In order to ensure that staff performance is maintained it is sometimes necessary to evaluate the **achievement** of employees. Performance management's primary goal is to maximise the performance of the individual, group or department and to achieve the goals of the organisation. An effective **performance management** system is a dynamic process, which changes as an organisation and its needs change.

Defining terminology

Before we begin, we need to clarify and define certain key terms:

Performance appraisal: A **performance appraisal** is a formal process used by the organisation to identify, measure and record an employee's job-related strengths and weaknesses.

Performance management: Performance management (also called reward management) is an organisation's strategies and policies to reward the employees in a fair and equal manner.

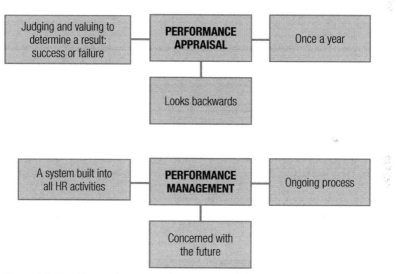

Figure 3.2 The difference between performance appraisal and performance management

---

DEFINITIONS

achievement – to accomplish something

performance management (reward management) – an organisation's strategies and policies to reward employees in a fair and equal manner

performance appraisal – a formal process used by the organisation to identify, measure and record an employee's job-related strengths and weaknesses

Personnel ratings

Personnel ratings are the measurements of an employee's work performance. They are observed and measured against a predefined standard or benchmark. Management keep a detailed record of the employee's performance. A value representing that specific performance will be measured against a standard performance.

Rating scales

A rating scale assists the human resources department to determine the quality of an employee's or a group's work performance. A rating scale determines how well an employee or group performs against defined standards.

Work standards

Work standards are usually recorded in a written description of how a task should be done. These standards manage consistent execution and provide a reference point for the performance of a task.

> **Key point**: A performance appraisal measures an employee's strengths and weaknesses. Performance management is a company's policies to reward employees.

Use of achievement awards

The major objectives of performance management are discussed below:

- To maintain records to determine compensation packages, wage structures, salary increases and promotions
- To recognise the strengths and weaknesses of employees
- To provide **feedback** to employees regarding their performance
- To assess the potential of employees to progress, grow and develop
- To motivate employees to achieve personal goals as well as the goals of the organisation
- To identify performance problems and to improve the performance of employees.

The performance appraisal process

Performance management is the continuous, systematic process of planning, assessing and reviewing of each employee's work performance. This process helps the employee to perform better and to develop their skills and knowledge.

Step 1:   Plan

This is the starting point. The planning phase involves not only management but also an integrated effort by management and employees. It is important to plan and determine which tasks the employee should complete, the results management expect and the methods that management will use to measure the employee's performance.

> **DEFINITION**
>
> **feedback** – the response to something, such as a product, process or an employee's performance to evaluate if it was successful or not

Step 2:   Setting performance objectives and measures
This might be the most difficult part of the process. The objectives and measurements need to be outlined in detail to include the full extent of the duties the employees should do.

The objectives and measurements need to be SMART:

Specific: clearly state who is responsible for each task as well as what and when tasks should be performed.

Measurable: define the objective in terms that can be measured, for example, quantity, quality, frequency, costs, deadlines.

Achievable: ensure the objectives and standards are possible to achieve by the person responsible.

Realistic: standards that are too high can overwhelm an employee. Standards that are too low do not push the employee to work hard, and can be demotivating.

Time-bounded: be clear about the time frame within which a goal is to be achieved. For example, "by the end of the day/week/month".

Step 3:   Monitoring and day-to-day coaching
The employee's performance must be continuously monitored for the performance management system to be effective. Day-to-day coaching by management is very important. Management will give employee(s) regular feedback about their work performance, their progress towards meeting the objectives or if any extra support is necessary. This also gives the employee(s) the opportunity to discuss and address possible concerns, issues and barriers for reaching the objective with management.

Step 4:   Formal performance review
Management do a formal performance review. The actual results of the employee's performance are assessed and then compared with the predetermined standards and objectives. Conduct formal appraisal interviews. Discuss any deviations and review standards and objectives to ensure that they are still realistic.

Step 5:   Final performance appraisal
This review is done once a year, usually at the end the year. Management then examines all their notes and/or any documentation that they used or completed during the year. They use these notes and documentation to assess the employee's performance more successfully. This is very similar to what management do in Step 4 but, in this case, the employees receive a final performance appraisal rating.

Step 6:   Forward appraisal rating to the human resources department
Every department head or manager is responsible for their department's performance ratings, but the human resources department is responsible for implementing the overall performance management system.

Power break 3.1 INDIVIDUAL WORK

Read the following paragraph and then answer the question:

> James is a sales representative at Sports Today, selling sports equipment and apparel. One day, James receives an email from Sheila Patel, the human resources manager, discussing his performance evaluation. James's performance was not good and he is not meeting his performance targets. According to his direct supervisor, James is not prepared to take on any extra work if required or to work weekends at sporting events to find new clients.

Questions:

1 Sheila has to apply the performance appraisal process, step-by-step, for James. Explain how she and James would apply each step in detail to make sure that with the next performance appraisal James will meet the required targets.
2 What possible obstacles could Sheila encounter during this process?

Problems in achievement evaluation

Consistency and fairness are very important during performance appraisals. If done incorrectly, the performance appraisal can do more harm than good. The goal of performance appraisals is to ensure that the employee grows and improves in the position they are in. Often managers make the mistake of only highlighting what has gone wrong, leaving the employee feeling demotivated.

Problems encountered in the performance appraisal system

Infrequent observations and discussions
When performance appraisal is not a continuous and regular event, the results are in many cases not a true reflection of the employees overall performance. Some employees might be going through a difficult time during the appraisals or working on a particularly difficult project, which could take away some of the more positive achievements earlier in the year. If appraisal and progress discussions are held more frequently, a better overall impression of the employee is formed.

"Your performance appraisal is based on the next 30 seconds. Go!"

Figure 3.3 Observations should happen regularly and with a minimum of stress.

Stress
A performance appraisal can mean a salary increase, bonus or promotion, so the stakes are high and this can cause some employees a lot of stress. When performance discussions are held more frequently, there are less likely to be any surprises when the final performance appraisal happens.

Leniency and strictness error

The performance standards that are set for employees might either be too low or too high. If standards are too low, employees will not be motivated to perform, and if they are too high, employees get demotivated because they feel that success is impossible.

System not updated

Today's environment is very dynamic, which means the performance appraisal system has to be updated to echo what is currently expected of a job. Goals cannot be changed or altered only annually anymore. If management do not update the goals, employees might be appraised on items that are not applicable to current situations or environments.

Administrative load

Supervisors and managers may see the performance appraisal process as an increase of their work load.

High costs

The cost for a performance appraisal system can be quite high. The money that management spends and the time they invest in the performance appraisal does not always translate to improved productivity.

The impact of teamwork

Performance appraisals in most cases focus on the individual's performance. What can happen in this case is that the employee will ignore the team or corporation's goals, but rather focus on their own performance to make sure they receive the necessary review.

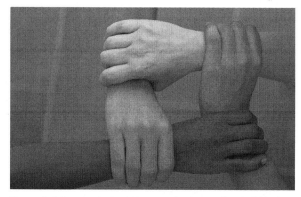

Figure 3.4 Teamwork should be appraised, as well as individual performance.

Management problems with employee performance appraisals

Ideally and in a perfect world, performance appraisals would be accurate and without any mistakes. Unfortunately, the reality is that managers doing performance appraisals can make common errors that will lead to inaccurate results. Let us consider some of these problems.

The recency effect

A common error made by management is that they focus too much or only on the employee's recent performance. They do not consider their previous results or performances. The entire period of employee performance must be evaluated otherwise the evaluation might be inaccurate. For example, a manager cannot only evaluate the last two months' performances and then ignore the rest of the year's performance.

Bias/subjectivity

Although performance appraisals should be objective, even with management's best intentions, each manager will bring their own subjectivity to the performance appraisal process. A manager might have a personal prejudice against a certain individual or group of employees. The evaluator's own values and norms may make them prejudiced against a certain group. This will influence the evaluation of employees who fall within those groups, which mean the results cannot be compared.

Similarity errors

Managers tend to give certain employees good ratings because they have something in common, or they have similar views. Managers should however focus on the outcome to make sure the employees achieve the desired results.

Generalisations (contrast errors)

The problem with generalisations is that an employee is rated according to the behaviour of a specific group and not according to their own behaviour. Management might generalise amongst people according to their race, religion, age or sexual orientation. Since the employee belongs to one of these specific groups, they are unfairly judged based on what is known about the group as a whole. An employee's performance should be rated, not their background, characteristics or lifestyle.

Ego effect

Some employees may have an inflated ego – a conscious positive feeling or belief about themselves. These employees might influence the way you feel about them. The error occurs when one employee is rated lower than the other because of the way the employee makes the manager feel. This is an example of ratings given based on an employee's likeability, rather than their performance.

Central tendency

Managers could rate employees wrongly because of the tendency to centralise ratings. They rate all employees as being average. Managers ignore differences between employees because they do not know their employees or they have too little information.

Halo effect

The halo effect causes one prominent factor to influence the rating of an employee, either positively or negatively. A "halo" is the ring you usually see around the head of an angel. The employee is rated on the basis of this one specific characteristic, while all other characteristics are ignored or overshadow by this characteristic. The rating is therefore either too favourable or too negative.

Figure 3.5 The Halo effect occurs when one factor influences how an employee is seen in general.

Performance appraisal tools and techniques

The following are the tools and techniques used by the organisation for performance appraisals of their employees:

Table 3.1 Performance appraisal tools and techniques

Performance appraisal tools and techniques	
• Ranking • Paired comparisons • Forced distribution • Essay method • Critical incident reports • Behavioural checklist	• Graphic rating scale • Behaviourally anchored rating scale (BARS) • **Management by objectives (MBO)** • Assessment centres • 360 degree appraisals

Ranking

With the ranking system, management ranks employees with all the other employees in similar positions within the organisation in order from the best to the worst overall performer. This is a very basic technique and it is suggested that it is used with a smaller number of workers.

The advantage of performance appraisal techniques is:
• It is a very simple and easy technique to use.

Disadvantages or limitations of this technique include the following:
• With the ranking technique it only gives the rank (number 1, 2, 3, etc.) of the specific employee. It does not show how much better or worse the one employee (for example, number 1) is compared to another employee (for example, number 2).
• This technique is not aimed at feedback to employees.

Paired comparisons

The employer compares each employee separately with each of the other employees. The employer compares the employees in pairs in similar positions, with a more highly rated and a less highly rated employee in every pair. The eventual ranking of an employee is then determined by the number of times they were judged to be better than the other employee. The ranking is based on overall performance of the employee (the skills, knowledge and time required). The successive evaluations will determine the order of the workers from the best to the worst.

A major disadvantage of this system is that the more employees there are to be ranked, the clumsier the technique becomes.

> **DEFINITION**
>
> **management by objectives (MBO)** – a personnel management technique where managers and employees decide together the goals for a specific period of time, e.g. a year or quarter

Example 1

Paired comparisons

Employees to be rated: John, Sipho, Claire, Tracy and Paul.

Employees rated → Performance compared with ↓	John	Sipho	Claire	Tracy	Paul
John	N/A	+	+	–	+
Sipho	–	N/A	+	–	–
Claire	–	–	N/A	–	–
Tracy	+	+	+	N/A	+
Paul	–	+	+	–	N/A

This table shows how employees compare to one another. The '+' indicates the better performer in each pair, and the '–' indicated the worse performer.

Employee	vs	Employee	Who's the better performer?
John	vs	Sipho	Sipho
John	vs	Claire	Claire
John	vs	Tracy	John
John	vs	Paul	Paul
Sipho	vs	Claire	Claire
Sipho	vs	Tracy	Sipho
Sipho	vs	Paul	Sipho
Claire	vs	Tracy	Claire
Claire	vs	Paul	Claire
Tracy	vs	Paul	Paul

This table shows which employee performs better compared with one other employee. It is another way of presenting the information in the table above.

Employee	Number of times chosen (+)	Rank
John	1	4
Sipho	3	2
Claire	4	1
Tracy	0	5
Paul	2	3

This table shows the final score or rank. Claire is ranked number 1; this means that she is the best performer. Tracy is ranked number 5, so she is the worst performer.

Forced distribution

The evaluator creates a number of categories for each performance factor (see Figure 3.6 below). Employees are then assigned to each of these categories, based on a percentage per category.

From the graph in Figure 3.6 we can see that the performance of most of the employees (40%) was average.

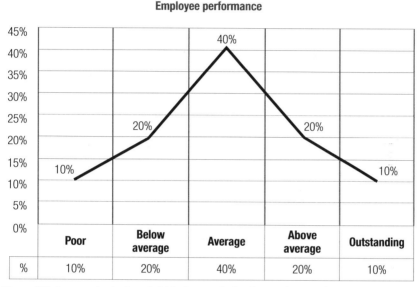

Employee performance

%	Poor	Below average	Average	Above average	Outstanding
%	10%	20%	40%	20%	10%

Figure 3.6 An example of a forced distribution graph showing employee performance

An advantage of the forced distribution method is:
* This technique eliminates bias ratings.

A disadvantages or limitation of forced distribution is:
* The employee's perception might be that they are very productive, but after they have been evaluated, they find themselves in a category way below their expectations. For example, the employee felt he should be in the 'above average' category, but after evaluation, he is in the 'below average' category. This might make the employee feel frustrated, decrease their productivity, cause low morale and increase absenteeism.

Essay method

With this method the person evaluating the employee writes a report for each employee they evaluate. It can be seen as a written essay that describes and discusses the strengths and weaknesses of the employee.

Bounce Media (Pty) Ltd

Employee Performance Appraisal

Suite 112
Private Bag X1257
JOHANNESBURG
0001

Phone: 011 – 554 1237
Fax: 011 – 554 1233
Email: info@bouncemedia.co.za

Name of employee: ....

Job title: ....

Department: ....

Attribute / Quality	Comments / Feedback
What does the employee do well?	
Which area should the employee improve to perform better?	
Describe any challanges that may influence the employee's performance.	
Discuss the employee as a member of a team.	
Describe the employee's leadership skills.	

Date: ....

Name of employer: ....

Signature of employer: ....

Figure 3.7 An example of a performance evaluation essay

An advantage of the essay method is:
- It is a valuable tool for feedback.

Some disadvantages or limitations are:
- The essay method is time consuming

- It is subject to personal preferences towards a certain employee
- The success of this method depends on the writing skills of the evaluator.

Critical incident reports

This technique requires the evaluator to continuously record actual job behaviours that are typical of success or failure as they occur. A certain behaviour of the employee can be seen as a critical incident. The behaviour can either be very effective or very ineffective. Both are seen as critical incidents, one positive (success) and the other negative (failure). At the end, these recorded critical incidents are used to evaluate the employee's performance. See Figure 3.8 below.

PureFit Construction

Critical Incidents

Name of employee: ....

Job title: ....

Date: ....

Continuing Duties	Targets	Critical Incidents
Schedule production for plant	Full (100%) utilisation of personnel and machinery	Instituted new production scheduling system
Order delivery on time	Decreased late orders by machine utilisation in plant	10% last month, increased by 20% last month
Supervise machinery maintenance	No shutdowns due to faulty machinery	Instituted new preventative maintenance system for plant: prevent machine breakdown by discovering faulty part

Supervisor: ....

Signature: ....

Figure 3.8 An example of a critical incident report

An advantage of a critical incident report is:

● This method provides the employee with thorough feedback of their performance.

Disadvantages or limitations include:

● This method is time consuming
● This method is difficult for the evaluator, because some incidents are more noticeable than others
● Negative (failure) incidents might, in some cases, be more noticeable than the positive (successful) incidents.

Behavioural checklist

This format provides the manager/evaluator with various descriptions of job-related behaviours. The manager/evaluator then has to indicate the employee's performance by choosing those behaviours which best describe their performance.

The manager or person evaluating responds to the questions by ticking the "yes" or "no" boxes.

Unifix Solutions – Cape Town CHECKLIST		
Name of employee:		
Job title (+ department):		
Date:		
Answer the following questions by ticking YES or NO.	**YES**	**NO**
1. Employee is a usual on the job.		
2. Employee maintains good discipline.		
3. Employee shows consistent behaviour towards co-workers.		
4. Employee keeps making mistakes.		
5. Employee shows preference towards particular co-workers.		

Figure 3.9 An example of a behavioural checklist

The advantages of using a behavioural checklist include:
- This is the most commonly used method in evaluation of the employee's performance.
- This method is behaviourally-based and not trait-based
- This is an acceptable and reliable method
- It prevents certain unwanted effects, for example, the halo effect.

The disadvantages or limitations of this method include:
- This method does not show the details of activities
- This method may have many items to check, making it time consuming.

Graphic rating scale

A graphic rating scale lists traits or characteristics required for the job. The scale indicates the degree to which the employee owns the specific trait or characteristic.

This is a very popular and frequently-used technique, which is based on job specifications. There are also many variations of graphic rating scales. The variations can be from the degree to which the points on the scale are defined or the dimensions on which individuals are to be rated.

Example 2

An organisation can use different ratings: a scale of 1–10; poor, average, or excellent; or does not meet expectations, meets expectations, or exceeds expectations.

A continuous scale shows a scale where the manager puts a mark on the scale that best represents the employee's performance, usually from poor to excellent.

Poor	Average	Excellent

GRAPHIC RATING SCALE

(TRAITS & DEGREE OF PERFORMANCE PRESENT)

Performance factors	Does not meet requirements	Partially meets requirements	Meets requirements	Exceeds job requirements
Quality of work				
Quantity of work				
Skills and experience				
Reliability				
Attitude				

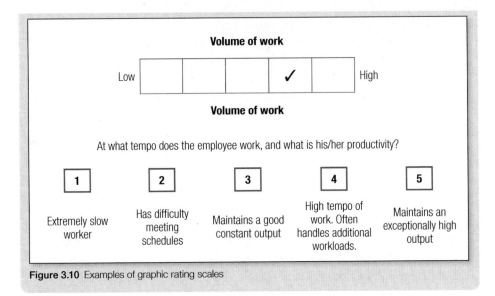

Figure 3.10 Examples of graphic rating scales

These are the advantages of a graphic rating scale:

- The scale is easy to understand
- You can compare individuals, because the rating is standardised
- It is less time consuming than other techniques.

The disadvantages or limitations include:

- This scale is subject to prejudice. It still depends on a person's perception
- This scale is not specific to the job itself but focuses instead on general behavioural qualities.

Behaviourally anchored rating scales (BARS)

The behaviorally anchored rating scale (BARS) method of evaluating employees conveys your typical job appraisals in a much more detailed way. You develop BARS for a specific job, and not for any position in an organisation. The BARS method bases appraisals on specific behaviours required for each individual position in an organisation.

This method requires a high level of participation from supervisors and/or managers. To develop a BARS, you need to have a thorough understanding of every position in the organisation's key tasks, as well as the full range of behaviours you expect from the individual to complete that particular task successfully.

You rate these specific behaviours for each employee; then you link each behaviour to a point on the scale. This point on the scale will indicate whether the employee's behaviour is exceptional, excellent, competent, or unsatisfactory.

At the end of the appraisal, management has a rating scale for each task. Figure 3.11 is an example of a BARS.

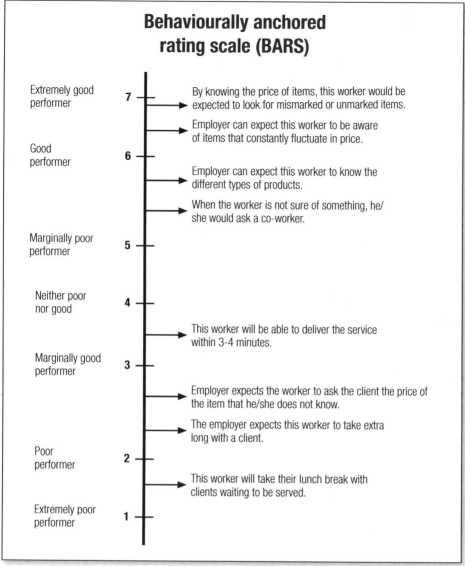

Behaviourally anchored rating scale (BARS)

Extremely good performer	7	By knowing the price of items, this worker would be expected to look for mismarked or unmarked items.
		Employer can expect this worker to be aware of items that constantly fluctuate in price.
Good performer	6	Employer can expect this worker to know the different types of products.
		When the worker is not sure of something, he/she would ask a co-worker.
Marginally poor performer	5	
Neither poor nor good	4	
		This worker will be able to deliver the service within 3-4 minutes.
Marginally good performer	3	Employer expects the worker to ask the client the price of the item that he/she does not know.
		The employer expects this worker to take extra long with a client.
Poor performer	2	This worker will take their lunch break with clients waiting to be served.
Extremely poor performer	1	

Figure 3.11 An example of a behaviourally anchored rating scale (BARS)

The advantages of a BARS are:
- This technique clarifies which behaviours represent good performance and which do not
- These behaviours are job specific
- The ratings reduce evaluating errors
- This technique promotes user participation.

Disadvantages or limitations:
- The BARS is a time consuming and expensive method to set up and maintain
- The BARS is job-specific and does not allow an organisation to use it across different jobs
- If the job requirements should change, a new BARS has to be constructed.

Management by objectives (MBO)

The concept of management by objectives (MBO) was first proposed by Peter F. Drucker in 1954 as a way of promoting managerial self-control.

Management by objectives is a personnel management technique where managers and employees decide together the goals for a specific period of time, e.g. a year or quarter.

The key to this method is the fact that management and the employee determine joint objectives. Management also provides feedback on the results. The employee participates in the decision-making. By setting challenging but achievable objectives, this method promotes motivation and the empowerment of employees.

Each individual personal goal is a building block towards the organisation's overall goal. Goals are set annually in writing. Managers will monitor the results on a regular basis to check the employee's progress. The rewards are based upon the employee achieving their goal(s).

The four elements of management by objectives (MBO)

1. Goal setting: goals must be objective, measurable, specific and understandable.
2. Participative decision-making: employees are part of the process of reaching goals of the organisation.
3. Time period: the time within which employees must accomplish their goals.
4. Performance feedback (assessment): this is where employees are measured against the preset standards.

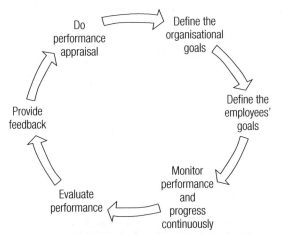

Figure 3.12 The six stages of the management by objectives (MBO) process

These are the advantages of the management by objectives (MBO) process:

- Management plan proactively and concentrate on the results, rather than just planning the activities
- The fact that employees participate in goal-setting encourages them to commit to work
- The MBO process clarifies each manager, department and employee's role
- Every employee knows exactly what to do and what he/she has to achieve. This makes control easy and effective.
- The goals are measureable, which make assessment easier and if necessary, it is easier to make adjustments
- The MBO process improves productivity, helps the organisation to gain efficiency and saves resources

- The MBO process increases employee motivation and the organisation's morale
- The MBO process gives employees a sense of personal satisfaction because they were part of setting the objectives.

The disadvantages or limitations of the MBO process include:
- The MBO process does not address the "how" of the performance, therefore it is unable to determine whether the achievements are really the outcome of individual excellence or of outside factors
- The MBO process can be time consuming and costly. It requires a great deal of administrative work and holding of meetings.
- There may be a lack of support from top management. Top management do not always like the fact that subordinates have equal opportunities to participate.
- Some subordinates may not like the idea of MBO. They may feel under pressure when objectives are set unrealistically high or too rigidly.
- Sometimes there is too much emphasis on reaching short term goals
- A number of managers do not have the necessary skills, knowledge and training with regard to interpersonal interaction that is required for MBO
- It is hard to uphold cohesion when the achievement of the goals of one department depend upon the goals of another department
- Both subordinates and managers have to feel comfortable with the process of MBO and both have to be willing to participate in it.

Assessment centres

An assessment centre's aim is to determine an employee's current managerial ability. Assessments consist of a standardised evaluation of behaviour. This standardised evaluation is based on multiple assessors and various methods, such as leaderless group discussions, simulations, ability tests and personality questionnaires.

The advantages of assessment centres include:
- Assessment centres appraise individuals' current managerial ability and not their past performances
- This method is quite suitable for development needs.

The disadvantages or limitations include:
- This method cannot be applied to all levels of employees
- The cost of the procedures is high.

360 degree appraisals

Employees receive confidential, anonymous feedback from the people who work with and around them. The assessments are made by supervisors, peers, subordinates and the employee themselves. This is a very effective appraisal tool and can also be seen as a development approach. The recipients gain insight into how other people perceive them and can use this information to improve their behaviour and/or performance. This is a well-balanced and thorough approach, because the employee is evaluated at all levels (horizontal – same level, vertical – up and downwards, internal – self, etc.).

Figure 3.13 360 degree appraisals

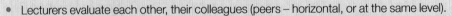

Example 3

A TVET college can apply the 360° appraisal as follow:

- Lecturers evaluate each other, their colleagues (peers – horizontal, or at the same level).
- The campus manager evaluates the lecturer (traditional – downwards).
- The lecturer evaluates the campus manager (subordinate – upwards).
- The lecturer evaluates themself.
- The lecturer evaluates the performance of the student administration office.

All the personnel at the TVET college evaluate or assess the people working with and around them.

Did you know? The different approaches to performance appraisals are sometimes understood to be the following: 360 degree appraisals, assessments by supervisors, peer ratings, self-appraisals and subordinate appraisals.

When conducting a 360 degree appraisal, all four types of appraisal listed below are incorporated:

Assessments by supervisors

This can be seen as the traditional approach or top-down appraisal. The manager or supervisor is the sole evaluator of their subordinates.

Peer ratings

This is the evaluation of the performance, or the quality of work, by a colleague or co-worker. This requires co-workers to have insight into one another's work performance.

Self-appraisals

A self-appraisal is very much as the name suggests. The employee determines their own level of performance or efficiency. This requires a degree of honesty and self-awareness.

Subordinate appraisals

Subordinate appraisals are an upward method of appraisal. The employees evaluate their managers. This means that employees are required to be honest and insightful about how their managers have performed.

The advantages of 360 degree appraisals include:

* The information is given as feedback to the employee, which then assists them to identify possible needs for career development
* This is a more balanced view of the employee's performance
* It helps with communication and the flow of information.

The disadvantages or limitations include:

* This method take a lot of time, and is complex in administration
* The exchange of feedback can cause trouble and tension amongst staff
* Employees may not feel comfortable offering honest feedback on supervisors
* An employee may not be completely honest in their evaluation, which can make it a subjective form of appraisal.

Power break 3.2   PAIR WORK

1 Get into groups of two. Revise Unit 3.1 and make sure you understand all aspects of performance appraisals and the various types of appraisals that are possible.
2 All organisations do performance appraisals at some time during the year. Visit an organisation of your choosing and study their performance appraisal process.
3 Ask your campus head or lecturer to write you a letter, explaining the purpose of the research and their appreciation for the organisation's willingness to accommodate you.
4 You and your partner are required to do a presentation of your research to the class.

Include the following in your presentation:

* What does the organisation want to achieve with their performance appraisal?
* What are the problems the organisation encounters during their performance appraisal process?

- What tools, techniques and/or methods does the organisation use for performance appraisals?
- What is your overall view of the organisation's performance appraisal process?
- What do you think they do well and where do you think they can improve?

Power break 3.3   INDIVIDUAL WORK

Read the following statements and identify the performance appraisals tools and/or techniques. Write only the tools and/or techniques next to the number (1–20).

1   You can compare individuals, because the rating is standardised.
2   This technique does not show how much better or worse one employee is compared to another employee.
3   The ratings reduce evaluating errors.
4   The behaviour of the employee can either be very effective or very ineffective.
5   The key to this method is the fact that management and the employee determine joint objectives.
6   This can be seen as the traditional approach.
7   The employee's perception might be that they are very productive, but after they have been evaluated, they find themselves in a category way below their expectations.
8   The employee determines their own level of efficiency.
9   This is the evaluation of the quality of work done by a co-worker.
10 Each individual personal goal is a building block towards the organisation's overall goal.
11 The successive evaluations will determine the order of the workers from the best to the worst.
12 The cost for the procedures is high.
13 With this method the person evaluating the employee writes a report for each employee they evaluate.
14 This is a very popular technique, which is based on job specifications.
15 This method requires a high level of participation from supervisors and/or managers.
16 The goals are measureable, which make assessment easier and if necessary, it is easier to make adjustments.
17 The employees evaluate their managers.
18 This method cannot be applied to all levels of employees.
19 This is a very effective appraisal tool and can also be seen as a development approach.
20 The evaluator then has to indicate the employee's performance by choosing those behaviours that best describe their performance.

UNIT 3.2 **Personnel compensation**

Compensation is very important to most employees. The economic exchange forms the basic component of any employment relationship. This revolves around the transaction between the employees and the organisation that employs them. When looking for a new job or getting a promotion, most people want to know how they will be compensated for their time and energy. Within the area of compensation there are two key concepts: reward management and employee compensation.

Reward management is the design or preparation and implementation of specific strategies and policies to reward employees. It is a whole system rather than a single idea. It is very important to reward employees fairly, equitably and consistently. In order to do this an organisation should have a reward management system.

Employee compensation means all forms of remuneration or reward that an employee might receive for work done, for example, salaries and wages.

> **Did you know?** The words compensation and reward have almost the same meaning in the context of personnel management.

Defining components of a reward management system

There are two separate categories of reward management; financial (monetary) and non-financial (non-monetary) rewards.

Financial rewards involve giving money directly to the employees. These are incentives given to employees of an organisation for worthy behaviour or for something they have done.

Non-financial rewards are forms of compensation that do not include money given to employees. Non-financial rewards are the benefits given to the employees of the organisation to increase employee job performance, employee loyalty towards the organisation, employee morale, and so on. Table 3.2 below shows examples of financial (monetary) and non-financial (non-monetary) rewards.

Table 3.2 Examples of financial and non-financial rewards

Financial (monetary)	Non-financial (non-monetary)
• Salary • Wages • Commission • Incentives • Bonus	• Promotion • Recognition • Job security • Job enrichment • Appreciation • Fringe benefits • Employee discounts • Flexi time • Paid sabbaticals • Day care

> **DEFINITIONS**
>
> **reward management** – an organisation's strategies and policies to reward the employees in a fair and equal manner
>
> **employee compensation** – all forms of remuneration or reward that an employee might receive for work done, for example, salaries and wages
>
> **financial rewards** – money that is given to employees
>
> **non-financial rewards** – the benefits given to the employees of the organisation to increase the employee job performance, employee loyalty towards the organisation, employee morale, etc. Not money given directly to the employees.

"The main requirement for this job is
the ability to live without money."

Figure 3.14 Remuneration is an important consideration for most employees.

Components of compensation administration

The importance of personnel compensation

Determining the rates of monetary compensation for employees is one of the most difficult and complex functions of personnel management. It is a very important function because of the significance for both the organisation and the employee.

There are a number of reasons for the importance of personnel (monetary) compensation:

* With money, employees can pay for basic necessities such as food and shelter.
* Monetary compensation is an important motivator and encourages employees to put in greater effort.
* Money serves as a source of status because money represents a measure of a person's worth and success.
* It allows the organisation to attract suitable new employees. If the wage and salary level are high enough, it will attract qualified persons to apply for open vacancies.
* It enables the organisation to hold their current work force. The organisation makes provision for promotions, salary increases and acceptable working conditions.
* Employees are motivated to prepare for and accept the greater responsibilities, demands and risks that go with higher-level positions. Higher remuneration convinces employees to compete for these advanced positions.

- It upholds equity in the organisation. Employees must feel that they are compensated fair in comparison to what others (internal and external) receive.

Different compensation formats

To understand the different compensation (or reward) formats better and to make the theory more practical, we are going start by studying the following example of a payslip. This is sometimes also called salary advice.

Pay Point	Personnel Number	Surname & Initials		Department	1
001/7801	5474712/AD04	Plaatjies, PK		Sales	
Identity Number		Job Title		Pay Date	
7601050012454		Assistant Sales Manager		2017/12/15	

2

TRANS ATLANTIC CONSTRUCTION

SALARY ADVICE

Tax Number	Number Of Medical Dependants		Pension Number	1
1122334456	Adults = 01	Children = 00	01234557	

Earnings	**3**	Amount	Deductions	**4**	Amount
Salary		18 171.75	Tax RSA		6 679.00
Commission		4 651.21	UIF Contribution		148.72
Bonus		10 000.00	Medical Aid		1 198.00
Cell Phone Allowance		452.25	-Employer 1 097.00		
			-Member fee 2 295.00		
			Parking		76.00
			CBDS Union		56.00
TOTAL EARNINGS:		**33 275.21**	**TOTAL DEDUCTIONS:**		**8 157.72**	5
Bank: Bank RSA	**Account Number:** 401155214		**Net Pay**		**25 117.49**	
Annual Leave:		**15.00**	**Sick Leave:**		**36.00**	6

Figure 3.15 An example of a payslip

The different aspects of the payslip are explained below:
1. Personal information about the employee: name, surname, identity number, personnel number, the department they are working in, tax number, the number of dependents and pension number. This payslip is for someone called PK Plaatjies, who is the Assistant Sales Manager.
2. The employer: In this example it is Trans Atlantic Construction.

3. The employee's earnings: These consist of a salary, commission, bonus and fringe benefits (cell phone allowance). As you can see, PK Plaatjies works in sales and earns commission.

4. The employee's deductions: From the salary advice you will see that the medical aid is on the "deduction" side. The employer and the employee make a contribution to the medical expense. The part that the employer pays is still seen as a fringe benefit.

5. The employee's nett pay: Before tax and other deductions, the amount of money an employee earns is called "gross pay". After deductions the amount of money is known as "nett pay", "nett wage" or "take-home pay".

6. The employee's annual and sick leave days: These are the days owing to the employee, meaning that an employee has not yet used up these days within this year.

> **Key point**: Compensation can include the following: salary, commission, bonuses, incentives and fringe benefits.

Salary

A **salary** is a fixed regular payment. Salaries are paid to employees at regular intervals, typically on a monthly basis.

Commission

Commission means a fee, normally a set percentage of the value involved, paid to a broker or agent for their service in facilitating a transaction. This form of remuneration is typical for sales employees.

In some organisations, a salesperson will receive a fixed base salary. The commission they earn above their salary is based on the number of items they sell. The employee will receive a percentage of the sales (e.g. 12%). In sales, base plus commission is the most common form of compensation.

> **DEFINITIONS**
>
> **gross pay** – the amount of money the employee receives before any taxes and deductions are made
>
> **nett pay (take-home pay)** – the amount of money the employee receives after all deductions, such as income tax and unemployment insurance (UIF)
>
> **salary** – a fixed amount paid at regular intervals, typically on a monthly basis
>
> **commission** – a fee, normally a set percentage of the value involved, paid to a broker or agent for their service in facilitating a transaction

Straight commission means the employee does not receive a base salary. The employee earns a percentage of each sale. The commission they earn is the only way to make money.

Bonus

A sum of money over and above an employee's normal salary as a reward for good performance is called a **bonus**.

Incentive bonuses are bonuses that are offered as an incentive, for example, a referral bonus. A referral bonus is given to someone recommending a potential buyer to the sales person, which leads to a successful sale.

Performance bonuses are bonuses given to employees as a reward for their outstanding and extraordinary work that they have done.

A reward bonus is a periodic payment over and above your normal payment, such as an annual bonus or 13th cheque.

Case study

Read the extract from the article and answer the questions below.

R877 000 bonus for SABC boss

12 November 2017

This week the SABC had some explaining to do regarding a discrepancy between a whopping R877 000 bonus for its acting group chief executive officer (CEO) Nomsa Philiso and the reason she claimed for being awarded the bonus. The SABC insisted that she earned it through hard work.

The SABC's annual report revealed that Philiso earned a total of R3.37m in the year ending March 2016. This included bonuses and commissions amounting to R877 000.

This all occurred while she was one of the public broadcaster's salespeople and long before she was appointed as CEO.

Acting SABC chief financial officer Thabile Dlamini told Parliament this week that the bonus came from an incentive scheme in the SABC's commercial enterprises division, which rewards staff who meet their targets.

However, while Dlamini told MPs that Philiso earned the money for heading the commercial enterprises division, it has been established that during the period for which she received the bonus, she was not heading the division.

Responding to this information on Friday, the SABC spokesperson explained that before Philiso's appointment as group executive for commercial enterprises in April 2015, she was the general manager for sales operations, a unit within the commercial enterprises division. This made her one of the employees in this unit who qualified for the incentive scheme.

to be continued...

> **DEFINITION**
>
> **bonus** – a sum of money over and above an employee's normal salary as a reward for good performance

Incentives

An **incentive** is a type of reward or payment to an employee to motivate or encourage someone to do something or to stimulate greater performances. In Unit 3.3, we will discuss incentives schemes in detail.

Fringe benefits

Fringe benefits are non-monetary forms of compensation that you would get in addition to your salary. These can include things like a company car, house allowance, medical insurance or pension schemes. On the payslip in Figure 3.15 a fringe benefit is the cell phone allowance.

Fringe benefits, sometimes called "perks", are given to an employee in addition to their wages or salary. These benefits can improve job satisfaction and help organisations to offer a competitive benefits package. Salaries are important, but human resources can use fringe benefits as tools to hire and retain top talent and to help create a motivated workforce. For example, medical aid has become very expensive and employees who may have previously left a job are more likely stay for these benefits.

There are different sorts of fringe benefits. Here are some examples:
- Pension
- Medical aid
- Life insurance
- Housing
- Car and transport allowance
- Child care benefits
- Relocation assistance
- Educational Assistance
- Cell phone allowance.

> **DEFINITIONS**
>
> **incentive** – a type of reward or payment to an employee to motivate or encourage someone to do something or to stimulate greater performances
>
> **fringe benefits** – a non-monetary form of compensation in addition to your salary, such as company car, house allowance and medical insurance

Power break 3.4 INDIVIDUAL WORK

Use the following information to create a payslip for an employee named Joshua Barkley.

Business name: Intel Technology Marketing

Employee name: Joshua Barkley

Job title: Sales director

Earnings for June 2018:

Salary: R15 221,54

Mid-year bonus: R 7 501,63

Commission: Joshua receives 12% commission on sales. He sold R28 000 worth of products this month.

Deductions for June 2018:

Income tax: R 4 448,08

UIF: R 148,72

Trade union subscription: R 73,45

Medical aid: R 1 235,12

Complete the payslip and fill in any detail that might be left out or not given. The more detail, the better.

Case study

Read about some of the benefits employees receive at Google. To get an idea of how they go above and beyond to make sure their employees are happy, compare the last benefit Google employees receive (New parents…) with our Basic Conditions of Employment Act (BCEA) and what we are entitled to in South Africa.

Google's best perks

Google has always looked after its staff, providing workers with a lot of benefits to make it worthwhile to stay with the company. We asked some Googlers which perks they liked best:

Free gourmet food. Google employees are extremely well fed, getting healthy and varied breakfast, lunch, and even dinner if they stay late – all for free! There are also coffee and juice bars dotted across campuses. Employees love this perk because, "it saves me time and money, and helps me build relationships with my colleagues."

Dogs are welcome! Googlers can bring their pets to work. A former employee describes why bringing his dog to work is so great. He says that it not only helped keep his energy up, but brought spontaneous joy to his co-workers and helped him meet people.

Googlers in Silicon Valley get a free ride to and from work. All the buses are equipped with Wi-Fi, so not only do employees not need a car to get to work, but they can relax or get work done on the way there.

to be continued…

Free "massage credits." Employees can give each other "massage credits" for doing their jobs well. The massage credits can be redeemed for a one-hour massage on campus.

New parents get a break. It's typical for mothers to get time off from work for up to six weeks after having a child in the US, but at Google it's a bit different. New dads receive six weeks of paid leave, and moms can take 18 weeks, plus employees' stock continues to vest (and they continue to receive bonuses) while they are on leave. According to one employee, "Google even gives us a bonus, bonding bucks shortly after our baby is born to help with expenses like diapers, takeout and formula during our leave." When parents return to work, there are free **daycares** for children on Google campuses.

Figure 3.16 Google employees can bring their pets to work.

Considerations in determining a compensation package

The total compensation that an employer offers to an employee, including bonuses, commission, salary and benefits, is known as a **compensation package**. There is a substantial amount of reasoning and negotiation involved in determining the compensation package, which includes the salary, of an employee. There are basic factors an organisation should consider before deciding how much to pay their employees:

- Supply and demand. If there is a decrease in supply of labour or a scarcity in a specific skill, the tendency is to compensate an employee more. The employer's need for labour means that they are willing to increase the compensation. The opposite will also apply.

> **DEFINITION**
>
> **compensation package** – the total compensation that an employer offers to an employee, including bonuses, commission, salary and benefits

- Legal considerations. There are laws that affect the compensation you pay in terms of minimum wages, overtime rates and benefits. The most important of these laws are as follows: the Labour Relations Act; the Basic Conditions of Employment Act; the Wage Act; the Compensation for Occupation Injuries and Disease Act; the Employment Equity Act and the Unemployment Insurance Act.
- Trade unions. The trade union's primary goal is to represent workers and try to maximise their wages and improve their working conditions. They will do this through collective bargaining with employers. A trade union's strengths and bargaining power depend on the number of employees or percentage of employees they represent. A high number of employees or a high percentage of representation gives them bargaining power to restrict the supply of labour to the employer and demand higher wages.
- Ability to pay. If the organisation is unlikely to be able to pay employees competitive salaries and wages, employees will look for positions where they get paid more. The success of the organisation will also play a role. A highly successful organisation does not have to pay the employee more than the competitive rate, because the success of the organisation makes it attractive enough to stay.
- Cost of living. Cost of living is the income any individual or household needs to be able to pay or afford the basics needs like housing, food, taxes and healthcare. As soon as prices on these necessities increase or decrease, it affects the cost of living, which in return will affect how an employee's income will be able to maintain their (and their dependents') standard of living.
- Compensation policy. An organisation's compensation policy will also influence the wages and benefits they pay. This policy provides the basic guidelines for salary increases, promotions, demotions, overtime, etc.
- Equity and its impact. This is the employees' need for equal compensation in comparison to other organisations (external).

Figure 3.17 The cost of living includes things like groceries, rent and basic necessities.

The basic process in wage and salary administration

Wage and salary management refers to the creation of a system to make orderly payments that are reasonable to both the employee and the organisation. The five basic processes are as follows:

1. Start by doing a salary survey to determine what other organisations pay employees in similar positions.
   - The organisation wants to determine whether or not their wages and salaries are on par with other organisations. Another way of saying this is that their wages are reasonable externally.

- A compensation survey gathers information and statistical analysis so that the organisation can determine how much they should pay their employees in specific positions.
- The information and statistics are for a specific position in a specific industry. Each industry is different. It is of the utmost importance that an organisation pays its employees fairly. If you pay employees inadequately, they will eventually leave to find a better offer. If you pay employees too much and the organisation's payroll budget and profitability will suffer.
- Organisations use market research to gather data about market related salaries. There are websites (for example: www.adtalent.co.za; www.payscale.com; www.careerjunction.co.za; https://mywage.co.za) that the organisation can use to gather the necessary information and statistics for a specific vacancy in a specific industry.

Power break 3.5   INDIVIDUAL WORK

Within the next year you might start to apply for vacancies and you will also do research about the market related salary for someone with the same qualifications, experience and industry as you. Some application forms and interviews require you to state your expected salary.

1 Visit the following website: https://www.payscale.com/
2 Use this website to answer the following questions:
   a) What is the median salary for a copy editor in Johannesburg?
   b) Compare your answer for question 1 with the median salary of a copy editor in Cape Town.
   c) Is there a difference between the salaries? If so, why?

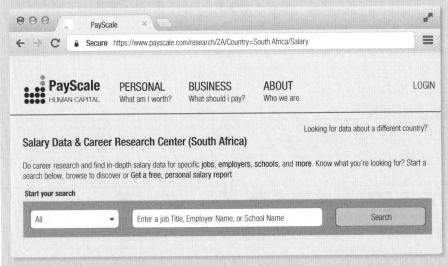

Figure 3.18 The PayScale website

2. Determine the worth of each job in your organisation.

   To determine how much each job is worth, the organisation will do a job evaluation. A job evaluation defines the relative value, for pay purposes, of jobs in an organisation. We will discuss job evaluation in detail in the next section.

3. Group similar jobs into pay grades.

   Just as you went from grade to grade in school, an organisation's compensation system is also divided into pay grades. You start at the bottom and work your way up. Each **pay grade** is worth a certain amount that an employee will receive. Every pay grade's worth is determine by the responsibilities of the position, the amount of authority of the position and the experience of the employee performing the job.

4. Put an amount or rate on each pay grade using wage curves.

5. Make the necessary fine adjustments to the pay rates.

The importance of determining a remuneration package in South Africa

A remuneration package is the whole package that an employee receives when they work for you. This includes things like salary, bonus, commission and fringe benefits. It is important to determine a fair remuneration package for employees regardless of the industry you work in. If you pay employees too little they will be demotivated, absenteeism might increase and staff turnover will increase too. In certain sectors of the South African economy, your workers might go on strike if they feel they are being paid too little. This is very disruptive and bad for productivity.

To determine a fair, realistic and market related remuneration package, the organisation will start off using job evaluation.

Power break 3.6   INDIVIDUAL WORK

1 Do a compensation survey. Search the internet or newspapers for the following vacancies:
   a) Legal secretary
   b) Sales manager.

2 Find three different advertisements for each of these positions to compare the salaries for the same position. Try to find vacancies from different parts of South Africa and different organisations.

3 Compile a compensation package. Choose either of the two roles (legal secretary or sales manager) and compile a compensation package for this role for an imaginary company. You can be as creative as you like (add perks such as free lunches or "casual days") but make sure your package is realistic. Ensure that the compensation package complies with South African labour practice.

4 Create an advertisement for the role and include details of the compensation package.

Job evaluation

Job evaluation is a method to decide the remuneration that should be paid to a specific job. Job evaluation determines how much each job is worth to the organisation. It consists of an official and systematic evaluation of jobs in order to decide what one job is worth relative to another job. The end result is a wage or salary hierarchy.

The easiest procedure of job evaluation is to compare the content of jobs in relation to one another. For example, compare the job's effort, responsibility, and skills. This information is then used to rank all jobs in an organisation. Job levels are established and a monetary pay range attached to it.

Did you know? The Code of Good Practice on Equal Pay for Work of Equal Value "seeks to promote the implementation of remuneration equity in the workplace by employers … through human resources policies, procedures, practices and job evaluation processes."

(See: Employment Equity Act, No. 55 of 1998)

The purpose of job evaluation

Job evaluation is done to:

- Eliminate personal prejudices in the evaluation of the relative worth of a job
- Develop a fair and comparable remuneration structure
- Provide management with the necessary guides to be applied in employee performance appraisals with regards to fair remuneration
- Collect the necessary information to determine recommendations required for selection, promotion, demotion, job changes or transfers
- Assist in setting wage rates or salaries for new job classifications
- Limit the bargaining issues with trade unions to realistic matters.

Job evaluation methods

Any job evaluation method, or job evaluation system, is based on factors that influence the remuneration of employees. This means that the outcome of the job evaluation method will determine an employee's salary. There are four basic methods of job evaluation that fall into two categories; non-quantitative and quantitative.

The non-quantitative method does not provide an exact, calculated number. It is an estimation, whereas the quantitative method results in an exact measurement.

- Non-quantitative methods consist of job ranking and job classification. Jobs are treated as a whole, and job descriptions, rather than job specifications, are often applied. This happens, for example, in government organisations.
- Quantitative methods consist of the points allocation system and the factor comparison method. Quantitative methods use a much more detailed approach. Job

factors are selected and measured. The organisation's job analysis programme must describe requirements for each of these factors. This happens, for example, in private organisations.

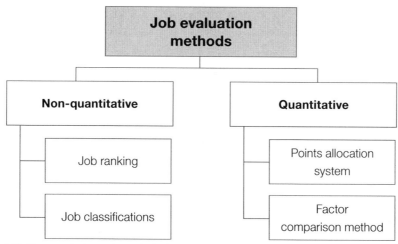

Figure 3.19 Non-quantitative and quantitative job evaluation methods.

The job ranking method

This is the process whereby jobs are ranked and compared to one another. Imagine you work in an organisation's human resources department. You need to make sure that the different jobs in an organisation have been identified. Compare each job with all the other jobs in the organisation and rank each job relative to all other jobs. The different jobs are ranked and compared in a hierarchy, which is based on the difficulty of the job.

The ranking method is the simplest, but least used method of job evaluation, because it is based on subjective views of the evaluator. For this reason, it can legally be challenged and it can become more and more difficult as the number of jobs increases.

Table 3.3 An example of job ranking

Ranking order	Annual remuneration scale
Managing Director	R960,000
General Manager	R707,497
Functional Manager (finance, marketing, etc.)	R344,516
Accountants	R253,128
Salesman	R217,490
Supervisors	R203,702
Secretaries	R121,170
Filing clerks	R95,271
Cleaners	R37,562

The job classification method

This is a basic and widely-used method. Jobs are arranged into groups. These jobs are classified together into categories that contain similar jobs. They will receive the same rate of pay instead of determining separate wages for each job.

Moving from one job classification to another constitutes a promotion. Every time an employee changes their work slightly, they move into a different rate of pay.

Category	Rank	Jobs (group)
1	Executives	Marketing manager, production manager, office superintendent
2	Skilled workers	Purchasing assistant, financial clerk
3	Semi-skilled workers	Typist, machine operator, filing clerk
4	Less skilled workers	Information desk clerk, cleaner, messenger

Figure 3.20 An example of classification

The points allocation system

If the organisation uses the points allocation system, it chooses factors that are present in all the jobs of the organisation and ranks these factors numerically.

This system involves four steps:

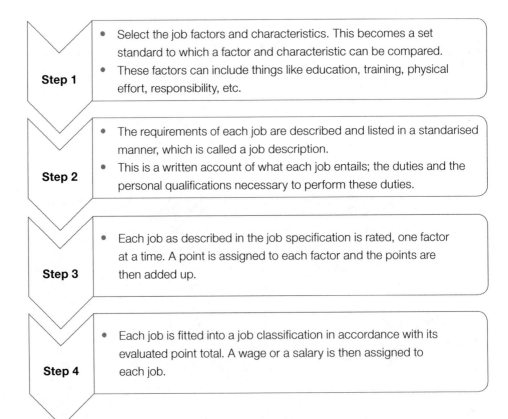

Step 1
- Select the job factors and characteristics. This becomes a set standard to which a factor and characteristic can be compared.
- These factors can include things like education, training, physical effort, responsibility, etc.

Step 2
- The requirements of each job are described and listed in a standarised manner, which is called a job description.
- This is a written account of what each job entails; the duties and the personal qualifications necessary to perform these duties.

Step 3
- Each job as described in the job specification is rated, one factor at a time. A point is assigned to each factor and the points are then added up.

Step 4
- Each job is fitted into a job classification in accordance with its evaluated point total. A wage or a salary is then assigned to each job.

JOB	RESPONSIBILITY				SUPERVISION				
	Education	Experience	Complexity of duties	Monetary	Contact with others	Type	Extended	Work situation	Total points
Typist	40	25	40	5	5	–	–	10	125
Telephone operator	40	50	40	5	20	–	–	10	165
Machine operator	60	100	60	10	10	–	–	15	255
Secretary	60	100	60	10	10	–	–	5	245
Cost accountant	80	125	60	40	20	20	5	10	360
Sales engineer	100	150	80	60	60	–	–	15	465

Figure 3.21 An example of the points allocation system

The factor comparison method

The factor comparison method is an enhancement of the job ranking method, which was already discussed. This method involves comparing jobs one by one, using the following five benchmark compensable factors:

1. Skill requirements
2. Mental requirements
3. Physical requirements
4. Responsibilities
5. Work situation.

A benchmark is a standard, or a set of standards, that the organisation can use as a point of reference for evaluating performance or level of quality.

The organisation establishes benchmark jobs or key jobs. A monetary value (wage or salary) is given to each factor. Then you determine the level of importance of each compensable factor that we find in each job by comparing it to the benchmarked job. At the end you attach monetary values to generate specific, compensated jobs.

The number of key jobs are determined by the size of the organisation or the number of jobs evaluated.

Key job	Skill requirements	Mental requirements	Physical requirements	Responsibilities	Work situation
Electrician	5	5	7	6	2
Fork lift operator	4	5	5	3	3
Inspector	6	8	6	7	6
Labourer	4	6	4	5	3
Clerk	5	8	4	6	6

Figure 3.22 An example of the factor comparison method

Case study

Read the following article and answer the questions.

Lecturers call job evaluation report "unfair"

30 July 2017
Kenya

Vice-chancellors of public universities have demanded an urgent meeting with the Salaries and Remuneration Commission (SRC) over a job evaluation report that has attracted protest from academic staff.

University academic staff union (Uasu) has rejected the evaluation that gives more recognition to administrative staff at the expense of those in the academic section despite having invested heavily in their education.

"We are rewarding staff in administrative positions, some with one degree, yet lecturers with three degrees are being rated below them. This is unacceptable," Dr Wasonga said.

Already several universities in the country are struggling to replace retiring lecturers who hold PhDs.

Vice-chancellors are ranked highest at E5, deputy vice-chancellors and principals of colleges are at E4 while the lowest ranked employee was a sweeper at grade A.

Associate professors who also hold doctorate degrees were ranked at E1 together with deputy librarians and finance officers, a level below registrars in universities.

Seniors lecturers at grade D4 have been put together with senior librarians, senior estate managers and bookshop managers, among others, with catering and hostels managers being above senior lecturers.

Senior lecturers are required to have a minimum of PhD with more than 15 years of experience at the university.

However, a transport and garage manager and a farm manager were ranked higher than a university lecturer. They were put in Grade D3 while a lecturer is at grade D2.

to be continued...

DEFINITION

compensable factors – factors (things) that you may receive compensation (payment) for

Job evaluation systems used in South Africa

There are a large number of evaluation systems in use in South Africa. We will discuss the following job evaluation systems: the Paterson system, the Peromnes system, the Hay and the Q methods.

The Paterson system

The Paterson system sees the employee's ability to make decisions as the most significant function. In all jobs, employees have to make decisions, which means the Paterson system can group jobs in similar categories according to their decision-making.

In an organisation with different functions, different types of decisions are taken on the various hierarchical levels depending on the intensity of the decision. These levels are decision-making bands that represents the various activities in the organisation. Each band is then subdivided on the basis of one additional "higher" or "lower" order factor. All levels, with the exception of unskilled workers, have two levels. The levels are further subdivided into sub-grades.

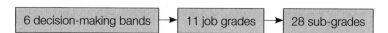

The Paterson system is widely used in South African organisations by the mining sector and sugar industries, amongst others.

Decision-making band		Job grades	Sub-grades
F	Policy formulating (Top management)	Higher F – co-ordinating – 11	F5
		Lower F – policy formulating – 10	F4
E	Programming (Senior management)	Higher E – co-ordinating – 9	E5
			E4
		Lower E – programming – 8	E3
			E2
			E1
D	Interpreting (Middle management)	Higher D – co-ordinating – 7	D5
			D4
		Lower D – interpreting – 6	D3
			D2
			D1

Decision-making band		Job grades	Sub-grades
C	Routine (Skilled workers and supervisory management)	Higher C – co-ordinating – 5	C5
			C4
		Lower C – routine – 4	C3
			C2
			C1
B	Automatic (Semi-skilled workers)	Higher B – co-ordinating – 3	B5
			B4
		Lower B – automatic – 2	B3
			B2
			B1
A	Defined (Unskilled workers)	Lower A – only defined – 1	A3
			A2
			A1

Figure 3.23 Paterson's job grading structure

The Peromnes system

The Peromnes system is the most frequently used job grading system in South Africa. It was developed by South African Breweries as a simplified version of another method, called the Castellion method.

The Peromnes system is a point system that evaluates jobs according to eight identified compensable factors:

1. Problem-solving
2. Consequences of error judgement
3. Pressure of work
4. Knowledge
5. Job impact
6. Comprehension
7. Educational qualifications
8. Subsequent training and experience.

These factors are considered essential requirements of a job. Every single job in the organisation is assessed against these eight factors and then given a numerical value to the description best explaining the character of the job. At the end, the total number of points will tell the organisation how much a specific job is worth.

Grade	Descriptions/job level example
1	Most senior executives and specialists nationally and other top management and very senior specialists
2	
3	

Grade	Descriptions/job level example
4	
5	Senior management, high-level specialists
6	
7	
8	Middle management, super intendants and low-level specialists
9	
10	
11	Supervisors, high-level skilled and clerical
12	
13	
14	Lower-level skilled and clerical
15	
16	
17	
18	Low-skilled and unskilled
19	

Figure 3.24 The Peromnes job grading system

The Hay method

The Hay method is a points-based, analytical system for evaluating jobs. The method is based on three compensable factors:

1. Know-how
2. Problem-solving
3. Accountability.

There are a total of eight elements that are applied to each factor. A complicated quantitative system is used to evaluate each factor and element of a task.

The main purpose of the Hay method is to put all the tasks in a hierarchical order from the most to least important and difficult.

In any job there will be a relationship concerning these three factors. Therefore, the final outcome or output you expect from a job (accountability) will require a particular level of input (know-how) and handling of this know-how (problem-solving) to be able to deliver the output.

This can be represented by the simple model:

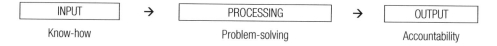

INPUT	→	PROCESSING	→	OUTPUT
Know-how		Problem-solving		Accountability

Factors		Elements	
1.	Know-how: the sum total of each type of skill necessary for acceptable work performance	1.1	Performance procedures: specialised techniques and knowledge in the occupational or commercial field or the professional or scientific discipline
		1.2	Width of management know-how
		1.3	Human relationship skills
2.	Problem-solving: finding a solution to a problem	2.1	The environment in which thinking takes place
		2.2	The challenge undertaken by the thinking
3.	Accountability and its results: the measured effect of the work on the end results of the organisation	3.1	Freedom to act: the extent of personal procedure or systematic guidance and control over actions in relation to the primary emphasis of the task
		3.2	Task impact on end results: the extent to which the task can affect thinking that is necessary to render results within the primary emphasis
		3.3	Extent: the portion of the total organisation that includes the primary emphasis of the task

Figure 3.25 The Hay method

Consequently, jobs can be differentiated by the size or level of each factor and also by the balance between the factors. For example, in an academic job (a lecturer or teacher), the evaluation will lean towards "know-how" and "problem-solving", while for a person in sales the balance moves towards "accountability".

The Q method
This system is also known as the questionnaire method. The Q method is a promising tool for conducting **formative evaluations**. The system is based on the idea that there is a direct link between the worth of a certain job to the organisation and the complexity of such a job.

Three principal factors are used to evaluate jobs according to this method:
1. Quality of decision-making is necessary for successful execution of a task.
2. Control will serve to qualify the decision-making competency.
3. Contact with people will determine the extent of the job incumbent's influence in the organisation.

Job structure	Total numerical ranking	Decision-making factor	Grades
Managing Director	158	135	Grade I
Technical Director	146	123	
Regional Manager	130	107	Grade H
Branch Manager	117	98	

DEFINITION

formative evaluation – the assessment in the development stage of someone's learning

Job structure	Total numerical ranking	Decision-making factor	Grades
Branch Secretary	112	89	Grade G
Chief Accountant	100	86	
Senior Technical Officer	95	73	Grade F
Accountant	82	72	
Personnel Officer	72	62	Grade E
Technical Officer	59	51	
Accountant Clerk	59	49	Grade D
Switchboard Operator	40	32	

Figure 3.26 The Q method

UNIT 3.3 Incentive schemes

An **incentive scheme** is a programme to encourage and motivate employees to work at their maximum capacity and to be as productive as possible. The employee who is incentivised will receive extra rewards for their good performance.

According to the International Labour Organization (ILO), incentives are "payment by results", however it is correct to call it the "incentive system of payment" since it places more emphasis on motivation. This means that incentives are awarded to workers for outstanding performances. This means that workers are encouraged and motivated to earn more by increasing their productivity.

Different kinds of incentive schemes

There are a number of different types of incentive schemes or motivational programmes available to employers. Here are a few examples of different incentive schemes:

Figure 3.27 Different types of incentive scheme

Piecework scales

This is the simplest system in use. The employee's payment is based on the number of "pieces" of work that a worker completes over and above a specific standard per time unit.

Piecework is divided into three different types; basic, or normal, piecework plans, the Taylor piecework plan and the group piecework plan.

Basic piecework plans

These are the normal piecework plans, which are the most basic and general incentive schemes. These plans depend on an established price per unit of production, which is based on time study and job evaluation.

Example 4

At a t-shirt manufacturing company, a standard has been established that an employee can produce 5 t-shirts per hour and their basic compensation is R10 per hour. The piecework is R2 per extra t-shirt produced.

Nadia works for 5 hours. She produces 50 t-shirts in 5 hours. This means she will produce 25 extra t-shirts (50 – 25) in the 5 hours. Her basic compensation will be R50 (5 hours x R10). The piecework is R2 per extra t-shirt, and so her incentive bonus will be R50 (2 x 25).

Figure 3.28 Nadia gets a piecework bonus of R2 per t-shirt.

The Taylor piecework plan

This plan, also known as Taylor's piece-rate system, is based on the degree of efficiency of the employee. The employee who exceeds the standard output within the given time frame must be rewarded with a high rate for their high production. The opposite also applies. The employee who fails to reach the level of output within the standard time should be paid a low rate.

Example 5

A cup manufacturer sets the standard rate at 50 cups per hour. R1 per cup is paid for up to 49 cups produced. When the employee exceeds 50 cups per hour, R2 per cup is paid.

This means that the employee earns R49 if she produced 49 cups (this is a low rate and the employee thus fails to reach the level of output).

However, she earns R102 (51 x R2) if she produces 51 cups (this is a high rate).

This strongly incentivises the employee to be productive because her payment is much lower if she does not hit the standard of 50 cups in one hour.

Power break 3.7   PAIR WORK

Velile is a carpenter at a furniture workshop. The workshop is owned by Mrs Baloyi who sells the furniture that Velile makes. The standard rate is 2 chairs produced in a day. He earns R50 if he produces 1 chair a day. For every chair over that, Velile earns R60 per chair.

1 What does Velile earn if he produces 2 chairs in one day?
2 What does Velile earn if he produces 3 chairs in one day?
3 Why would Mrs Baloyi want Velile to work quickly?

Group piecework

Sometimes employees who work in a group cannot be evaluated individually, such as in certain sectors of the production industry. Therefore, the payment is based on the combined output of a number of workers, rather than on the output of each worker individually. If production is lower or equal to the set standard, the normal compensation is paid to the group. When the production exceeds the set standard, a group bonus is paid, which is divided equally between the members of the group.

Example 6

A group of employees are all responsible for the manufacture of cell phones. The standard rate is set at 5 cell phones per hour. If 5 cell phones per hour is exceeded, the group is paid their normal rate plus an incentive bonus of 3 units.

If the rate for one cell phone is R10, that means an incentive bonus will be 3 x R10 = R30 per hour to the group. This must be split equally amongst the members of the group.

Time bonuses

Time bonuses are based on the time standard and not on the production standard. Bonuses are calculated according to the time saved.

Bonuses based on time saved

The Halsey plan
The Halsey plan ensures that the wages of time saved are shared by workers and employers, so this method helps to reduce the labour cost per unit. In the Halsey plan, a standard time is set for completing a job and an hourly rate is then determined. If a worker takes more than the standard time to complete a task, they will be paid according to the time rate, i.e. time taken multiplied by the rate per hour.

In the case of the worker finishing the task in less time than the standard required, he/they will be paid according to the actual time, i.e. time rate, plus the bonus. Generally the bonus is a percentage of the saved time.

Example 7

The usual bonus share paid to the worker is 50% of the time saved multiplied by the rate per hour (time rate). The standard time is 8 hours and the rate per hour is R2.

Person A takes 10 hours. His earnings: 10 hours x R2 = R20

Person B takes 6 hours. Her earnings: 6 hours x R2 = R12

> Plus a bonus of R2/hour x 2 hours saved x 50% = R2.

Thus, Person B's total earnings are R14 (time wages + bonus), if she has completed the work in 6 hours, less than the standard time.

The hundred percent time premium plan
In working conditions where it is possible to determine accurate time standards an employee can be paid the full value of the time saved.

For example, Person B in Example 4 will then receive R4 (R2 x 2 hours saved) bonus.

The Bedaux plan
This plan is based on a bonus of less than 100% of the money involved in the time saved. This means that a percentage of the time saved is paid to the employee concerned while the rest of the money is divided between the employees who contributed in some way to finish the task in less time.

Bonuses bases on time worked

The Rowan plan
This plan is based on the competence of the employee's execution. The employee who performs more efficiently than the standard determines receives an incentive bonus.

The Emerson plan
The Emerson plan is also based on an efficiency percentage, like the Rowan plan. According to this plan, an employee is guaranteed to receive their daily wage regardless of how they perform. The standard output is set as 100% efficiency and is fixed. The standard time for completing a task is then compared to the actual time it took the

employee to complete the task. The efficiency of the employee's performance can be calculated by dividing the time it took the employee by the standard time.

According to the Emerson plan the employee will be paid the time rate up to an efficiency of 67% (66.66%). This percentage is equal to 2/3. Any performance better than 67% means that the employee will be paid a bonus. At 100% efficiency, the worker is paid time wages, plus a bonus of 20% on the wages earned.

A bonus percentage is linked to the efficiency percentage according to a sliding scale. According to this sliding scale, 100% efficiency earns a bonus of 20%. It will increase by 1% on every 1% increase in efficiency.

Example 8

Standard output in 10 hours = 200 units. Rate per unit = R2

Person A's output in 10 hours is 100 units. Her efficiency = 50% (100/200 x 100). As efficiency is below 67% the worker is only entitled to time wage, thus, earnings = 10 x R2 = R20.

Total earnings = R20

Person B's output in 10 hours is 200 units. His efficiency = 100% (200/200 x 100). As the efficiency is 100%, Person B is paid time wages, plus a bonus of 20% on wages earned. Earnings: Time wages = 10 x R2 = R20
Bonus = 20/100 x R20 = R4
Total earnings = R24

Bonuses based on standard times

The Gantt task and bonus plan
The standard time is fixed for completing a task. This standard time is based on a time and motion study. The employee's actual performance is measured against the set standard time to decide how efficient they were. The employee will be paid accordingly.

An employee performing below 100% efficiency will only receive their time wages. Performances over and above 100% efficiency will receive the standard time wage plus a bonus on the wages they earned.

Figure 3.29 Bonuses are based on a time standard and not a production standard.

Profit sharing plans

According to these plans, employees will receive a pre-set share of the profits of the organisation.

Profit sharing plans can be divided into:

- Current profit sharing

Employees are directly paid their share of the profits in cash or stock. This may occur either monthly or quarterly.

- Deferred profit sharing

Shares that the employees received are held in a trust and are only released on retirement, death, permanent disability or other stated circumstances.

- Combination profit sharing

This plan is most often used in medium-sized organisations. This plan compromises of the current and the deferred plans.

Employee share ownership plan (ESOP)

The ESOP provides the employee with interest (ownership) in the organisation. It is an employee-owner programme. Organisations offer the employees stock ownership. This is often without any upfront cost for the employees. The shares given to the employee are part of their remuneration for work done.

The shares distributed to the employees may be held in an ESOP trust until the employee retires or decides to resign. The employee then has the option to either sell it back to the company for redistribution, or it is cancelled.

Sales incentives

Employees in sales are subject to predetermined sales targets. This refers to the minimum amount of products they have to sell per month, which is set by the employers.

Sales incentives are rewards given to employees who sold more than the minimum requirements. The manufacturers of certain products also reward sales of their particular product as part of a promotion. The same principle of a predetermined target applies. Sales incentives can be in different forms, including cash or special prices or rewards, such as a paid holiday at a glamorous or exciting destination.

The purpose of incentive schemes
The purpose of incentive schemes is to:

- Boost the morale of employees. With everyone rewarded for accomplishing the organisation's goals and displaying organisational values, morale will drastically increase.
- Generate productivity and revenue. When your employees are engaged, they are more productive, making your revenue stream bigger.

- Foster teamwork. Collaboration and innovation are key elements to a business's success. Engagement will open lines of communication and foster effective teamwork for the benefit of your company.
- Motivate employees. When employees are aware of the incentive schemes that are in place at their organisation, they know that the extra effort, energy and time they put in on the organisation's behalf will be acknowledged and rewarded.
- Improve the performance of the employee. The incentives will not only motivate employees to put in the extra effort, but it will also make them strive for better overall performances. For example, they will begin to provide superior service to the clients.
- Retain trained and skilled employees for the organisation.

Figure 3.30 Incentives help to motivate employees to reach their goals.

The advantages of incentive schemes
The advantages for employees are:
- participation in the benefits of the organisation
- higher standards of living
- higher measure of need satisfaction
- job satisfaction.

The advantages for employers are:
- a high level of productivity, which results in higher profit and efficiency
- a decrease in personnel because of higher productivity
- a reduction in the cost of training because trained employees are retained.

UNIT 3.4 Termination of service

The function of separation, otherwise known as **termination of service**, can be as complex and challenging as any other human resources function. Termination is when an employee's relationship with the employer ends and they separate.

It is very important that the organisation establishes a policy with regard to termination of service. The policy is designed to provide certainty and consistency when the time arrives for termination of services. The policy should include issues such as the notice period, responsibilities, procedures, termination on certain grounds, termination without cause, termination initiated by employees, etc. For both the employee and the employer it is very important to also comply with the terms of the service contract, and, if applicable, with the terms of a trade union agreement.

There are two main types of job termination; voluntary and involuntary.

- Voluntary termination of employment by the employee is when the employee chooses to leave the job they are employed at.
- Involuntary termination means that the employee's contract is terminated by the employer.

Termination refers to any kind of separation between the employee and the employer, for example, if the employee gets a better job and leaves their current job, they terminate their contract. This is sometimes known as "quitting". **Dismissal** is a type of involuntary termination. It is also known as "being fired".

Termination of service and dismissals will be discussed in detail in Labour Relations N5.

Termination of service by the employee

Voluntary termination may include the following:

- Resignation
- Retirement/pension
- Death.

Resignation

There are a number of reasons for employees to resign. Here are some examples:

- The employee is offered a higher paying job
- The employee needs a new challenge

> **DEFINITIONS**
>
> **termination of service** – any kind of separation between the employee and the employer
>
> **dismissal** – the involuntary termination of service, also known as firing

- The employee is looking for a more flexible schedule
- Personal circumstances, such as moving overseas.

The employee needs to submit a letter of resignation detailing when the **resignation** is effective from, according to the employment contract. The contract would normally say what the **notice period** is.

The notice periods according to the Basic Conditions of Employment Act, Section 73 are shown in Table 3.4 below:

Table 3.4 Notice periods according to the BCEA

The employee is employed for:	Notice period:
6 months or less	One week
More than 6 months, but less than 1 year	Two weeks
1 year or more	Four weeks

The personnel department should hold an exit interview in the case of any kind of termination. The purpose of the exit interview is to:
- Help management determine the reason behind the resignation
- Minimise misunderstandings and resentments
- Complete administration.

Did you know? A letter of resignation is a brief, formal business letter informing an employer that the employee is resigning from a job. Regardless of the reasons for resigning, the letter should always be written in a polite and professional tone because you should maintain positive relations with the company.

Retirement and pension

At what age should an employee retire? Should it be 55, 60 or 65? There are no hard-and-fast rules. The Basic Conditions of Employment Act does not prescribe an exact age at which employees must retire. The **retirement** age is typically determined by the employer and stipulated in the contract of employment. As soon as the employee signs the contract, they agree to a specific retirement age.

DEFINITIONS

resignation – when an employee decides that they will not continue working at the company or organisation

notice period – the time period the employee gives the employer when they resign This is time between the resigning and the last working day.

retirement – when an employee stops working, usually because the person reaches a certain age

"How long is it now until your retirement, Pamela?"

Figure 3.31 Many employees look forward to retirement.

Death

Termination due to death can be of natural causes or an accident. As soon as the human resources department receives the unfortunate news that an employee has passed away, they will:
* send the organisation's condolences in writing to the immediate family
* determine any outstanding salary and leave due to the deceased and will advise the payroll department to make the necessary payment.

Termination of service

Termination of service at the initiative of the employer can occur when the employee is not fulfilling the job requirements and the situation cannot be improved through training. It can also happen when the business can no longer retain all its employees as a result of unfavourable economic and financial circumstances, or when disciplinary action needs to be taken against an employee.

Dismissal, firing or discharging

Dismissal (also referred to as firing or discharging) is the termination of employment by an employer against the will of the employee, It is the most serious and rapid way of ending an employer-employee relationship.

The employee is dismissed from their job for a specific reason. The reasons can be for serious misconduct by the employee, such as inadequate performance, ethical or legal violations, failure to follow company rules and regulations, breach of contract, theft, forging documents, violence, harassment or threatening behavior towards others, gross insubordination, and so on.

Retrenchment

Retrenchment is a process whereby the employer has to assess its business needs in order to increase profits or limit losses. This leads to reducing its employees to cut labour costs. It is an unfortunate situation for the employees, because they did not do anything wrong.

It is important for the employers to consider alternatives for retrenchment. They must consult with all the relevant parties as soon as they consider retrenchment. If there is no alternative to retrenchment, the organisation has to follow fair procedures.

Medical boarding

Medical boarding means the employee is no longer able or medically fit to do their job. Before an employee is boarded, the employer should explore the possibility of alternative employment appropriate to the employee's capacity.

Only in circumstances where the employee can no longer perform in the position and the employee is unable to be accommodated with alternative employment, may the employer terminate the employment relationship. The employer should give the employee reasonable notice.

Figure 3.32 Medical boarding occurs when an employee cannot perform in their position and no alternative employment is available.

Problems with regards to termination of service

Terminating the services of an employee is never an ideal situation for an employer to find themselves in. In the list below, you will see just a few issues that arise as a result of employees' services being terminated, whether this is voluntary or involuntary:

- High costs involved with the recruitment of new employees
- High costs involved with the training and induction of new employees
- Loss of productivity during the recruitment process
- Higher wastage for new employees
- Loss of skilled, experienced employees
- Higher risk of accidents with new employees
- Hired equipment not fully utilised during the recruitment process
- Problems meeting delivery dates.

WHAT DO WE KNOW AND WHERE TO NEXT...

Revisiting the learning objectives

Now that you have completed this module you should have achieved the learning objectives listed in the table below:

Learning objective	What you have learned	Tick box
Differentiate between terms regarding employee achievement such as performance appraisal, personnel ratings, rating scales and work standards.	**Definition of employee achievement terms:** A **performance appraisal** is a formal process used by the organisation to identify, measure and record an employee's job-related strengths and weaknesses. **Personnel ratings** are the measurements of an employee's work performance. A **rating scale** assists the human resources department to determine the quality of an employee's or a group's work performance against defined standards. **Work standards** are usually recorded in a written description of how a task should be done.	☐
Explain the use of achievement awards in practice.	**Use of achievement awards:** • To maintain records to determine compensation packages, wage structures, salary increases and promotions • To recognise the strengths and weaknesses of employees • To provide feedback to employees regarding their performance • To assess the potential of employees to progress, grow and develop • To motivate employees to achieve personal goals, as well as the goals of the organisation • To identify performance problems and to improve the performance of employees.	☐
Describe potential problems related to performance appraisal which may prevent its effectiveness in practice.	**Problems in achievement evaluation:** • Infrequent observations • Stress • Leniency and strictness error • System not updated • Administrative load • High costs • The impact of teamwork.	☐

Learning objective	What you have learned	Tick box
Differentiate between different achievement evaluation techniques and methods used in practice in South Africa.	**Different achievement evaluation techniques/methods:** • Ranking • Paired comparisons • Forced distribution • Essay method • Critical incident reports • Behavioural checklist • Graphic rating scale • Behaviourally anchored rating scales (BARS) • Management by objectives (MBO) • Assessment centres • 360 degrees appraisals.	☐
Define basic terms regarding remuneration such as nett wages, take-home pay, salaries, commission, bonuses and fringe benefits.	Definition of remuneration terms: **Nett pay (take-home pay)** is the amount of money the employee receives after all deductions, such as income tax and unemployment insurance (UIF). A **salary** is a fixed amount paid to an employee at regular intervals, typically on a monthly basis. A **commission** is a fee, usually a set percentage of the value involved, paid to a broker or agent for their service in facilitating a transaction. A **bonus** is a sum of money over and above an employee's normal salary as a reward for good performance. **Fringe benefits** are non-monetary forms of compensation in addition to your salary, such as a company car, house allowance and medical insurance.	☐
Explain the reason for the importance of personnel compensation in the work environment.	**Components of compensation administration:** • With money employees can pay for basic necessities such food and shelter. • Monetary compensation is an important motivator and encourages employees to put in greater effort. • Money serves as a source of status because money represents a measure of a person's worth and success. • It allows the organisation to attract suitable new employees. If the wage and salary level are high enough, it will attract qualified persons to apply for open vacancies. • It enables the organisation to hold their current work force. The organisation make provision for promotions, salary increases and acceptable working conditions. • Employees are motivated to prepare for and accept the greater responsibilities, demands and risks that go with higher-level positions. Higher remuneration convinces employees to compete for these advanced positions. • It upholds equity in the organisation. Employees must feel that they are compensated fair in comparison to what others (internal and external) receive.	☐

Learning objective	What you have learned	Tick box
Explain the basic processes in wage and salary administration in a pragmatic way.	**The basic processes in wage and salary administration:** • Start by doing a salary survey • Determine the worth of each job in your organisation • Group similar jobs into pay grades • Put an amount or rate on each pay grade by using wages curves • Make the necessary fine adjustments to the pay rates.	☐
Describe the different components of a personnel compensation system briefly.	**The different components of a personnel compensation system:** • Salary • Commission • Bonus • Incentives • Fringe benefits.	☐
Compile a compensation package according to principles used in the South African labour practice.	See page 111	☐
Discuss the nature and purpose of job evaluation in practice.	**The nature and purpose of job evaluation is to:** • Eliminate personal prejudices in the evaluation of the relative worth of a job. • Develop a fair and comparable remuneration structure. • Provide management with the necessary guides to be applied in employee performance appraisal with regards to fair remuneration. • Collect the necessary information to determine recommendations required for selection, promotion, demotion, job changes or transfers. • Assist in setting wage rates/salaries for new job classifications. • Limit the bargaining issues with trade unions to realistic matters.	☐
Describe the different job evaluation systems briefly.	**A summary of the job evaluation system:** 	☐

Learning objective	What you have learned	Tick box
Explain how job evaluation data is used to develop the pay structure of an organisation.	Job evaluation systems used to develop the pay structure in South Africa: • The Paterson system • The Peromnes system • Hay method • Q method.	☐
Differentiate between different kinds of incentive schemes used in practice in addition to the basic wage structure.	**Different kinds of incentive schemes used in practice in addition to the basic wage structure:** • Piecework scales • Time bonuses • Profit sharing • Employee share ownership • Sales incentives.	☐
Indicate the purpose and advantages of incentive schemes in the effective management of a compensation policy in practice.	**Incentive schemes in the effective management of a compensation policy:** • Boost the morale of employees • Generate productivity and revenue • Foster teamwork • Motivate employees • Improve the performance of employees • Retain trained and skilled employees for the organisation.	☐
Discuss the procedures to be followed in the case of the termination of service of an employee and the problems which are experienced in this regard.	There are voluntary or involuntary termination procedures to be followed. **Voluntary termination includes:** • Resignation • Retirement • Death. **Involuntary termination includes:** • Dismissal • Retrenchment • Medical boarding. **The problems with termination are:** • High costs involved with the recruitment of new employees • High costs involved with the training and induction of new employees. • Loss of productivity during the recruitment process • Higher wastage for new employees • Loss of skilled, experienced employees • Higher risk of accidents with new employees • Hired equipment not fully utilised during the recruitment process • Problems meeting delivery dates.	☐

Assessment

True or false questions

Choose whether the following statements are TRUE or FALSE. Write only the number of the question followed by 'true' or 'false'.

1. Take-home pay is the amount of money that the employee receives after deductions.
2. Sales incentive schemes are in the form of commission based on sales and they also share in the profit of the organisation.
3. Dismissal and termination of services are synonyms.
4. Commission is a set percentage of the value involved in a transaction.
5. The Taylor plan for incentives is based on the time saved.

(5 x 2) [10]

Multiple choice questions

Choose the correct answer from the various options provided. Choose only A, B, C or D and write your answer next to the question number:

1. Which one of the following is NOT a financial reward?
   A   Wages
   B   Daycare
   C   Bonus
   D   Incentives   (2)
2. Identify which one of the following is a fringe benefit:
   A   Bonus
   B   Incentives
   C   Flexi-time
   D   Child care.   (2)
3. The Hay method can be represented by a simple model. Identify which one of the following is incorrect:
   A   Output = Accountability
   B   Input = Know-how
   C   Input = Processing
   D   Processing = Problem-solving.   (2)
4. An employee can produce 10 units of a specific product per hour and their basic compensation is R15 per hour. The employee produces 100 units in 5 hours. their basic compensation will be R75 (5 hours x R15). What will their piecework per unit and incentive bonus be?
   A   R2.00
   B   R1.75
   C   R1.50
   D   R1.25   (2)
5. Use the Paterson system and the table below to determine which of the jobs below got the 3rd most points.

JOB	Responsibility				Supervision				
	Education	Experience	Complexity of duties	Monetary	Contact with others	Type	Extended	Work situation	Total points
Cleaner	10	15	15	5	15	–	–	10	70
Financial clerk	50	95	50	25	20	10	5	10	265
Mechanical engineer	80	100	80	5	10	–	–	15	290
HR Manager	65	90	65	10	25	–	–	15	270
Sales Manager	60	100	65	50	25	–	–	10	310

    A   Financial clerk

    B   Mechanical engineer

    C   HR Manager

    D   Sales Manager   (2)

    (5 x 2) [10]

Short questions

Briefly answer the following questions:

1. Explain how a performance appraisal could be conducted using a traditional approach. (5 x 1)

2. Except for the traditional approach to performance appraisals, name any THREE other approaches. (3 x 1)

3. List the processes of termination of services under the following headings:
   a) Termination initiated by the employer (3 x 1)
   b) Termination initiated by the employee. (3 x 1)

4. Explain the term reward management. (3)

5. Explain what management by objectives (MBO) is. (3)

    [20]

Long questions

Answer the following questions as comprehensively as you can:

1. One of the concerns about performance appraisals amongst employees is the "potential pitfalls with regard to the system or method" used during the performance appraisal process. State the EIGHT aspects that could go wrong during the performance appraisal process. (8 x 1)

2. Why would employees prefer to receive incentives as a method of payment? (5 x 2)

3. Name the factors that form the basis of the Peromnes method of job evaluation. (8 x 1)
4. List any FIVE advantages of management by objectives (MBO). (5 x 2)
5. Organisations need to evaluate the performances of their staff at least once a year. Why is it necessary to do this? (6 x 2)
6. Inform staff about the process management will follow to evaluate their performance. Name and briefly explain each step. (6 x 2)
7. Name and explain FIVE basic considerations in determining a compensation package. (5 x 2)

[70]

Grand total: 110 marks

MODULE 4

QUALITY OF WORK LIFE

This module covers the following:

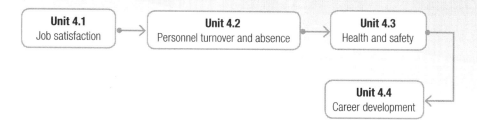

Unit 4.1
Job satisfaction

Unit 4.2
Personnel turnover and absence

Unit 4.3
Health and safety

Unit 4.4
Career development

Learning objectives

By the end of this module, you should be able to do the following:

- Explain the impact of job satisfaction and its relationship to worker productivity/ effectiveness and commitment
- Explain how job satisfaction of employees can be measured or assessed by management
- Explain major causes of job satisfaction in practice
- Indicate the relevance of job enrichment to job satisfaction
- Review the influence of job rotation as a method of training for job satisfaction
- Demonstrate how to measure absenteeism and labour turnover and the cost thereof in practice
- Describe the factors which exert an influence on employee absenteeism and labour turnover in practice
- Describe methods of countering personnel turnover and absenteeism
- Recognise the importance of employee health with regard to employee effectiveness in practice
- Explain the importance of health and family care benefits and retirement benefits as part of a remuneration package (see incentive schemes)
- Briefly discuss the implications of substance abuse in the workplace
- Briefly describe the meaning of career development in the work environment
- Discuss in a pragmatic way the importance of career development to both employers and employees

- Briefly explain the responsibilities of the employee and the manager with regard to career development in practice
- Briefly explain some career development opportunities provided by South African organisations
- Explain a practical strategy for management to ensure effective career development.

Key terms

absenteeism	job enrichment	personnel turnover
career development	job rotation	productivity
career management	job satisfaction	safety risks
job enlargement	morale	substance abuse

Starting point

Julian Zipho, the human resources manager, and the organisation's top management all realise that money and rewards are not always going to motivate employees to be productive or committed to their jobs. A higher salary and more bonuses will only motivate an employee up to a point. Sooner or later the employee will get used to that additional income and look at other ways to stay motivated.

Other factors, such as quality of work life, job satisfaction, employee development and health and safety all play a part in keeping employees motivated and satisfied at work. Julian and his human resource team work very hard at ensuring that all of these elements are present in the workplace.

Figure 4.1 It is important for staff to stay motivated in their work environment.

UNIT 4.1 Job satisfaction

In the past, employees had very little input in management decisions. Management used to see employees merely as machines that worked and did not have to think at all. The job was viewed as nothing but a means to earn a living. However, this approach to management and towards personnel changed over time as a number of behavioral scientists conducted studies in this field. Over the years, **job satisfaction** has become increasingly important to employees and employers.

Flash back to N4: In Personnel Management N4 you were introduced to Maslow's Hierarchy of Needs. Do you remember the different levels? Physiological needs, safety needs, love and belonging, esteem and self-actualisation. Job satisfaction is related to the top two levels: esteem and self-actualisation.

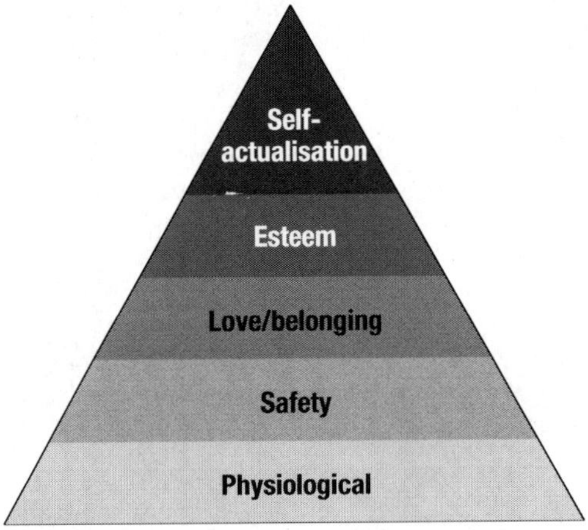

Figure 4.2 Maslow's Hierarchy of Needs

Job satisfaction is one of the factors that enables employees to perform at the highest level. This means that job satisfaction helps workers to be productive and committed to their work. In the current work environment more and more serious efforts are made to make employees' work more interesting and meaningful, to assist them in obtaining the right equipment to do their work, to provide more information on the work, to grant employees more authority and to create opportunities for them to develop personally and professionally.

Employees spend a lot of time at work and the quality of a person's work life is of the utmost importance to them. If employees are happy and satisfied at work they are more likely to be productive and motivated. In Table 4.1 below we have listed some positive and negative elements of a work environment.

DEFINITION

job satisfaction – the employee's contentment/satisfaction with their job or with particular aspects of the job

Table 4.1 Positive and negative elements of a work environment

Positive work environment	Negative work environment
• Democratic leadership	• Autocratic leadership
• Challenging work	• Uninteresting work
• Good communication	• Work stress
• Training and development	• Lack of recognition
• Healthy working conditions	• Poor working conditions
• Team effort	• Absence of team work
• Work autonomously	• Lack of trust
• Equal and fair treatment	• Victimisation and discrimination

When employees work in a negative environment it will start to affect productivity. This means that the employee will produce work that is not of as high a quality as if they were working in a suitable environment.

Example 1

John is an office assistant. He gets an above average salary and the company has given him a bonus for the last two years. Since a new manager has taken over, he is struggling to get the support that he had before. The manager constantly second guesses everything he does. He has also been forced to move to a small office without windows or air conditioner.

John's working conditions changed for the worse, and he is not allowed to work on his own. John became increasingly frustrated with the situation, influencing his productivity negatively and he is starting to look around for another job.

Did you know? In a survey conducted by Human Sciences Research Council (HSRC), it was found that:
• For most working South Africans, job security is the most important aspect of a job.
• Workers appear more satisfied with their job content than the ability of their job to secure their material needs.

Key point: Job satisfaction is important because it helps employees to be more productive and to feel committed to their work.

Measuring job satisfaction

Employees may seem happy on the surface and tell you that they are satisfied with their jobs. But are they really happy and satisfied?

There are a number of ways that employers can measure job satisfaction. Gauging job satisfaction can be informal or formal. Informal measurements could be the direct manager's weekly or monthly staff meetings in which managers can check what the overall feeling in their team or with individuals is. However, if the manager is not approachable or if the employees feel their concerns will not be heard, then the feedback the employees give will not be a true reflection of their job satisfaction. A more formal way of gauging job satisfaction is through an employee survey.

Figure 4.3 Employees who are satisfied in their jobs are engaged and find it easy to participate.

Factors influencing job satisfaction

There are a number of factors that determine job satisfaction and the factors may be different from person to person. For one person monetary benefits may be a more important factor to job satisfaction than a feeling of belonging at a workplace. Below you will find a list of factors that can influence job satisfaction.

Monetary benefits

Fair pay is crucial. You can enjoy your work and be truly happy and satisfied with your job, but that would not matter if you do not get paid according to a certain standard.

Appreciation

Everyone enjoys getting praised or being appreciated. Praise and appreciation will motivate employees, which will be displayed in their productivity and efficiency.
The more management appreciates employees, the more they will be satisfied with their jobs.

Fair treatment

Fair and consistent treatment are crucial to job satisfaction. There is not much worse than an organisation treating one employee different to another or rewarding them differently for doing the same work. On the opposite side of the coin, fair treatment will lead to satisfied employees, better performances and trust in management.

The feeling of belonging

It is natural to feel a need to belong. An employee who feels that they are part of the team have a much higher chance of job satisfaction.

Adequate working conditions

Good working conditions, with the necessary resources available, increase levels of job satisfaction. Employees need conditions that are healthy, safe, comfortable and conducive to being productive in the employee's particular field. Working conditions have a profound effect on job satisfaction.

Figure 4.4 A mine worker (left) and office workers (right).

Case study

Mine workers face difficult conditions

People working in mines in South Africa work under difficult and sometimes dangerous circumstances. Here are some headlines and short extracts of the news coverage that have dealt with working conditions in mines in South Africa:

Mining company's stocks fall after deadly mine accident

May 2018

Shares were down 7.7% in Monday afternoon trade on the JSE. This follows after 13 mineworkers were trapped underground on Thursday at Sibanye-Stillwater's Masakhane shaft in Driefontein, following two seismic events. Seven workers were killed and six of the surviving employees are in a stable condition in hospital, according to the mining company.

Mine safety has become a human rights issue - AMCU

May 2018

The Association of Mineworkers and Construction Union (AMCU) says mine safety has become a human rights issue. The union also says that legislation should be strengthened to hold mining bosses criminally accountable for failing to ensure safe working conditions. This follows after seven workers lost their lives after being trapped underground Sibanye-Stillwater's Masakhane shaft on Thursday due to seismic activity. Six other mine workers were hospitalised, and according to AMCU, four were in the Intensive Care Unit (ICU) and two others were critical.

Initiation and leadership
Giving employees equal opportunities to lead and display initiative will increase job satisfaction. This shows the employee who management trusts them.

Stability
Employees will not be happy and satisfied if the organisation changes things constantly. People want stability and job security.

Safety and security
Safety and security go hand in hand with working conditions, as discussed earlier. If an employee feels physically safe and secure at the organisation, the level of job satisfaction will increase. Job security means the employee's job is secure and that they will receive an income every month, which will also increase the level of job satisfaction.

Challenges
Some employees like to be challenged. They see it as a motivation and an opportunity to display their skills and abilities. They feel management trusts their capacity to fulfil expectations. This will improve their job satisfaction.

Responsibilities
Giving an employee more responsibility serves two distinct purposes. The first is that added responsibility suggests that management trusts the employee and their ability to handle the responsibility.
Secondly, and this links with the previous bullet, more responsibilities can be seen as a challenge. Both will increase the level of job satisfaction.

Creativity
Creative freedom gives the employee a sense of fulfilment. The employee might feel a personal connection with the job because their creativity was put into it, which in return increases the level of job satisfaction.

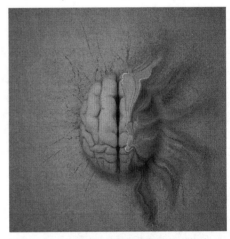

Figure 4.5 Having the freedom to be creative in the workplace increases job satisfaction.

Did you know? A recent survey of hundreds of professionals in America discovered some interesting insights about factors influencing job satisfaction.
- Growth = happiness. The more opportunities for growth in the organisation, the happier employees report to be.
- Flexible work hours were rated the third most important benefit.
- A third of the employees said their work environment is toxic and needs to change.
- Just over a third of the employees said they only receive feedback once a year or not at all. Most of the time they have no idea if their work performance improved or if they need improvement.

In Module 3, we read about the benefits employees receive at Google on a daily basis. Read the extract below from another article about working life at Google and answer the questions that follow.

The problem with too much freedom

March 2018

For some people, Google sounds like paradise. The company offers on-site daycare and gyms, free gourmet food and drink and even advanced Japanese toilets. But its biggest and most attractive benefit may be the high level of personal autonomy that Google allows its workers to have.

As one former Google employee explains, Google gives engineers almost unfettered creative freedom. Even Google says it, "hire the smartest people and they'll figure out what to do."

Autonomy

Most employees want more autonomy. This means being responsible for your own work and having the ability to make big decisions that affect you and your team. People who have a sense of control over their work report better job satisfaction, which means less stress, lower staff turnover, and more productivity.

On the other hand, employees with absolute creative freedom can end up feeling like a superhero, which can lead to over-the-top displays of entitlement. This entitlement may show itself in small daily events, like the squabbles that occur between workers over free food. But there are larger issues at play too. Over time, workers became less focused on the company's mission, and more interested in their individual career advancement. In other words, the company culture of enormous freedom starts to breed selfishness.

The middle ground

It is still true that employees are more likely to be creative and happy in their roles when they are in charge of their own work life. The key is to give employees the right amount of autonomy. They should have enough that they feel keen to work and be innovative, but not so much that they become self-involved and forget that their job has responsibilities, which sometimes entails doing stuff you would prefer not to.

Explaining the social purpose of a job can also reduce selfishness and entitlement. People are more willing to work on a boring project if they understand that there is a bigger purpose to the project. Job satisfaction is also about doing work that has meaning, not just being in total control of the work you do.

Questions:

1 Name the two most prominent factors influencing job satisfaction that were discussed in the article.

2 What are the benefits of a high level of job satisfaction mentioned in the article?

3 What is the downside to creative freedom, according to the article?

Job enrichment

Job enrichment can be defined as the purposeful restructuring of an employee's job to make it more challenging, meaningful and interesting. It increases the depth of the employee's involvement in the organisation. The employee will do their own planning, implementation and assessment of the job. The employee is able to do their job at a higher level.

It is important to note that there is a difference between job enrichment and **job enlargement**. These differences are explained in Table 4.2 below:

Table 4.2 The difference between job enrichment and job enlargement

Job enrichment	Job enlargement
Restructuring a position to make it more challenging, meaningful and interesting	Added duties and responsibilities that are not in the current job description
Used to motivate staff by expanding the quality and quantity of the job	Focused more on an increased workload
Employee takes on more responsibilities as a way to improve job efficiency and to facilitate career growth	Could be as a result of restricting or retrenchment that the employee needs to take on more tasks

Requirements for job enrichment

For an employee to react favourably to job enrichment, the following conditions are necessary:

- The specific employee must want to be part of job enrichment
- The employee should be consulted before implementation so that they can propose suggestions
- Employees must understand the job in its entirety
- The job must be meaningful so that the employee feels they are is performing an important task
- Employees must have independence and freedom so that they can make their own decisions in the job
- The job must offer variety, which means that a number of different skills will be used
- Management has to offer chances and opportunities for employees to grow and develop
- There must be feedback on the job they are doing.

> **DEFINITIONS**
>
> **job enrichment** – the purposeful restructuring of an employee's job to make it more challenging, meaningful and interesting
>
> **job enlargement** – added duties and responsibilities that are not in your current job description

The advantages of job enrichment

Job enrichment has the following advantages. It:

* Teaches new skills
* Boosts energy of the employee by reducing boredom
* Creates positive and better working environment
* Improves the decision-making ability of the employee
* Increases the chances of recognition and reward
* Provides motivation for advancement
* Provides a sense of accomplishment
* Reduces absenteeism
* Lowers staff turnover
* Creates a professional approach.

Figure 4.6 Job enrichment improves the decision-making ability of the employee.

The disadvantages of job enrichment

Job enrichment has the following disadvantages. It:

* Increases the employee's work load
* Makes additional skills necessary
* Can lead to a lack of knowledge
* Can lead to the employee not being able to handle the work pressure or work load
* Can lead to miscommunication
* Can lead to a lack of performance
* May not be approved by trade unions.

Job rotation

Job rotation means employees are transferred from job to job on a systematic basis. The employee gets the opportunity to experience all the different jobs, phases or parts of the organisation. Each job's duration can last from two weeks to six months.

The advantages of job rotation

* Job rotation gives some variation to the job and prevents the employee from doing the same thing over and over, which leads to boredom.
* It exposes the employee to a wider experience and gives them some insights into the entire organisation.
* Job rotation will help management to see the employee's skills, abilities and competencies.
* Management will get the opportunity to determine the talent of the individuals and what they do best.
* Management will have more certainty where to utilise the employee and where the right place is for them to excel.
* Job rotation turns specialists into generalists.
* It is an advantage for management because the employee can perform a variety of tasks.

> **DEFINITION**
>
> **job rotation** – employees are transferred from job to job on a systematic basis

- Job rotation builds the employee's self-belief, confidence and self-image.
- Employees will be more motivated and ready to handle new and different challenges.
- Employees will also be more flexible. They will be able to adapt more easily if a situation changes.

The disadvantages of job rotation

- Employees are only moving from job to job at the same level, which means it is the same type of job. That might cause frustration.
- The regular moving from job to job causes interruptions and breaks in the work procedure of the organisation.
- Employees have a tendency to take up a lot of time becoming familiar with new jobs and/or processes.
- Management wastes a lot of time in convincing and motivating employees towards job rotation.
- Job rotation increases costs and decreases productivity.
- Just as an employee becomes effective and efficient at their station/job, they have to rotate to a new one.
- The constant change can cause stress and anxiety. Not all employees enjoy being taken out of their comfort zone.
- An employee who is interested in a particular job and has to go through the rotation process might become demotivated.

UNIT 4.2 Personnel turnover and absence

In this section, we will be looking at personnel turnover and work absence, also referred to as absenteeism. Both of these have a negative impact on the organisation and are generally a symptom of there being a problem with job satisfaction. We will look at personnel turnover first and then move on to absenteeism and see how this can be combated.

Personnel turnover

Personnel turnover (also called staff turnover or labour turnover) refers to the number or percentage of workers who leave an organisation and are replaced by new employees. If companies have a high staff turnover, with new employees starting and then leaving soon after, it could be an indication that something is going wrong within the organisation.

> **DEFINITION**
>
> **personnel turnover** – (also called staff turnover, labour turnover) the number or percentage of workers who leave an organisation and are replaced by new employees

Did you know? High turnover costs more than you think.

Most people know that high employee turnover rates come at a cost for companies, however, very few discuss the true extended costs and the multiple ways that it impacts the business. That is why it is important that successful businesses not only find the best employees but keep them engaged as well.

Case study

How to keep employees happy and productive

One out of three employees are disengaged at work, according to a recent study. Here are the key findings from the study:

1 Employee engagement correlates with workplace satisfaction
   The more engaged your employees are, the more satisfied they will be with their working lives, and vice versa. This means that there is a clear relationship between workplace satisfaction and the level of employee engagement. Employees who are highly satisfied with various aspects of their workplace also demonstrate higher levels of engagement. According to the study, only 19% of workers in South Africa are highly engaged and highly satisfied at work.

2 Being engaged at work means having more control at work
   While employees like to have flexibility, companies are lagging behind this trend. In order for employees to be engaged and feel in control, companies need to realise that people want the freedom and control to work from anywhere.

The study shows that companies usually offer employees twice as much fixed technology as opposed to mobile technology. A fixed desktop doesn't match the way we work today. Employees don't have to go to the office to work; they prefer to work wherever they are. This means that companies need to give people the tools to work from anywhere.

The causes of personnel turnover are divided into two categories: **Avoidable** and **unavoidable causes** of personnel turnover. The table below shows just a few examples of these.

Table 4.3 Some examples of avoidable and unavoidable causes of personnel turnover

Avoidable causes	Unavoidable causes

• Employee resigns because of:
  – Dissatisfaction with job
  – Dissatisfaction with remuneration
  – Bad working conditions.
• The organisation can change its behaviour and how it deals with staff to prevent employees from leaving.
	• Employee leaves because of:
	  – Retirement
	  – Death
	  – Disablement
	  – Retrenchment.
	• The employer has no power over the employee leaving.

Case study

Read the following article and answer the questions.

"You're fired!" Trump administration experiences highest staff turnover in modern times

March 2018

President of the United States, Donald Trump, has seen a higher staff turnover than any other administration in the last century. Washington has been rocked by frequent reassignations, firings and resignations since Trump came to power in January 2017. In this time, almost 50% of Trump's staffers have been shifted, ousted or resigned.

Secretary of State Rex Tillerson was fired by tweet, a favourite mode of communication with the President, and former Secretary of Health and Human Services Tom Price was dismissed when his extravagant taxpayer-funded travel spending came to light.

Kathryn Dunn Tenpas, a senior fellow at Brookings Institution, a major Washington think tank, says that especially high rates of turnover increases disruption and inefficiency, deprives the administration of outgoing officials' political connections and personal networks, and can have a domino effect, as aides and assistants to the staffers who are exiting often follow them out.

Questions:

1 According to the article "almost 50% of Trump's staffers have been shifted, ousted or resigned". What does this statement mean?
2 How was Secretary of State Rex Tillerson fired?
3 Is this a formal mode of communication or not?
4 Why do you think high staff turnover affects efficiency?
5 How could the Trump administration reduce its turnover?

Formula for calculating personnel turnover

Personnel turnover (labour turnover) rates refer to the number or percentage of employees who leave the organisation over a particular period. The number refers to how many staff member left the organisation. For example, in a company of 170 people, 17 people left the organisation in 2017. The percentage is the number of staff who left the organisation in relation to the total number of staff members. In the example we gave, the percentage is 10% (17 of the 170). So 10% of staff members left the organisation in 2017.

There are different reasons for an organisation wanting to calculate personnel turnover. The organisation may want to check how many new employees leave within the first year of employment, perhaps after a major change that happened in management structure or operations, or to gauge employee satisfaction.

To calculate the turnover rate, you divide the number of employees who left by the number of employees at the beginning of the period. You can then further divide this number into voluntary and involuntary turnover.

Example 2

The organisation has 100 employees at the start of the year. During the year six employees quit and nine are retrenched late in the year.

The voluntary turnover rate for the year would be 6/100 × 100 = 6%

The involuntary rate for the year would be 9/100 × 100 = 9%

The total turnover rate would be calculated at 15/100 × 100 = 15 % (15 is the total amount of employees who left)

Power break 4.2   GROUP WORK

Desperado food trucks serve Mexican food at festivals all over the country. They have 10 different food trucks, and the company employed a total of 72 personnel at the start of 2017. In this year, 16 people resigned from their jobs with Desperado, saying that they were overworked and underpaid. In the same year, 5 people were dismissed for subordination and for lateness.

1 Calculate the turnover rate for Desperado in 2017.
2 What is the voluntary turnover rate?
3 What is the involuntary turnover rate?
4 Do you think their turnover is high or low?
5 Do you think Desperado food trucks will do well in future? Why?

The cost of personnel turnover

The higher an organisation's staff turnover rate, the higher the costs will be in finding and retaining the best employees. As the turnover rate increases, the costs will increase.

Hiring new employees comes at a cost. Every time an employee leaves voluntarily and needs to be replaced the organisation will incur costs. These include things such as:

* The cost of recruiting a new employee, which includes advertising, interviewing, screening and hiring.
* The cost of training and induction for the new employee.
* A new employee is not 100% productive at the beginning. It might take some time for the employee to become as productive as the employee who left.
* Co-workers or prospective employees who see an organisation with a high staff turnover tend to disengage and lose productivity.
* New employees are not as familiar with procedures and might make service errors.
* Employees may feel demoralised. They have to do extra work to cover for those who left, which means longer hours, overtime, late evenings, early mornings and time away from their families. Management can also ask them to train new employees, while they are still responsible for their own work.
* Employees who leave the organisation may disrupt the cultural set-up. The organisation might hire temporary staff who do not fit in with the organisational culture.
* Facilities will be under-utilised until a replacement is employed.
* There is usually an administration cost due to notifications and payroll changes.

Figure 4.7 Having employees stop and start continuously can cost the organisation.

The factors that cause personnel turnover

If you are seeing a high turnover rate among your business's personnel, it's time to consider what factors might be prompting the mass departure of your staff. The list below highlights some of the factors that cause personnel turnover:

Dissatisfaction with wages

Employees have to make a living and to be able to afford their basic needs. If an organisation only pays the minimum wages or low wages, employees may be dissatisfied and leave the organisation.

Dissatisfaction with working environment

It is the right of the employee to expect good working conditions. This includes things like proper lighting, adequate ventilation, good sanitary conditions, etc.

Dissatisfaction with the job

An employee not challenged by their job, or faced with the unavailability of their preferred job might decide to leave. This also applie to dangerous, noisy, dirty, oily, wet and smoky jobs, which may cause them to leave the organisation.

Dissatisfaction with personnel policies

Policies, such as dictatorship, no room for career development, transfer and leave requests being denied, all cause an increase in staff turnover.

Lack of medical, recreational and other facilities

The well-being of the employee is very important. Sufficient medical and recreation facilities in the organisation are important for the employee's health.

Lack of transport facilities

Transport is a big issue in South Africa and some employees live far away from work. Not all employees have their own transport. Many have no other choice than to use public transport – taxis, trains or buses – which are not always very reliable. This will cause employees to look for vacancies closer to home.

Dissatisfaction with working hours

If employees are requested to work extended hours with no overtime payment, they may decide to leave.

Absenteeism

Absenteeism is the failure of employees to report to work, or staying away from work without good reason or permission. But absenteeism does not only refer to employees not reporting for duty, it also includes arriving late and leaving early, extended breaks or attending to private business during working hours.

Figure 4.8 Not being productive at work is also seen as absenteeism.

An organisation can save a lot of money by evaluating and controlling absenteeism better. It is the employee's duty to be present at work and to deliver a certain level of service. This level of service is called **productivity**. The employer has the right to expect the employee to be at work and to be on time. In return, the employer will reward the employee for their services.

Formula for calculating absenteeism

When we address absenteeism in an organisation it is useful to have data to refer to. Perhaps absenteeism seems bad because there are so many empty desks or because productivity is low. But how do you quantify this? In other words, can we assign a value to absenteeism

> **DEFINITIONS**
>
> **absenteeism** – the failure of employees to report to without good reason or permission
> **productivity** – level of achievement, results or creativity

There is a mathematical formula that can be used in order to calculate the absenteeism percentage in an organisation.

$$\frac{\text{Total hours/days employees are absent}}{\text{Total hours/days worked}} \times \frac{100}{1}$$

We always multiply a number by 100 over 1 in order to get a percentage. This percentage will then be useful even if we are comparing it to absenteeism in a much larger or smaller company.

Example 3

A printing company called Colourific employs 54 full-time staff. During the second term (April, May and June), staff members were absent for 20 days in total. This could mean that 20 people each missed one day, or 10 people missed two days each, or any other configuration. Across the whole company, 20 working days were missed.

Everyone at Colourific works five days a week (Monday to Fridays), eight hours a day.

Number of employee hours lost through job absence in a specific period:

20 days × 8 hours = 160 hours

Number of working days in a specific period (Mondays to Fridays):

21 (April) + 23 (May) + 21 (June) = 65

Number of working hours:

65 days × 8 hours = 520

$$\frac{160 \text{ hours}}{(65 \times 8)} \times \frac{100}{1}$$

= 30.77%

The **absentee rate** for Colourific for the time-period in question is 30.77%.

The cost of absenteeism

While employers make provision for employees not being at work through annual leave, sick days and family responsibility leave, there will still be unexpected disruptions in employees work lives. For example, one of your employees may need an unexpected operation and an extended recovery period. This will have an effect on your productivity, as well as revenue. Remember that these are simply the days that the employer can count as the employee not being at work, which does not take into the account the days that an employee comes to work but does not actually do any work.

DEFINITION

absentee rate – the percentage of the organisation's total staff that is absent for a particular period of time

The cost of absenteeism includes the following:

- Cost for replacement of workers
- Overtime pay for employees who get scheduled when others do not show up
- Lack of productivity when no replacement is found
- Poor quality of products or services
- Stress for other employees who need to work longer hours
- Safety issues due to employees who are poorly trained to cover for those who do not show up
- The administrative cost of managing absence
- Cost of late deliveries and dissatisfied customers.

The factors causing absenteeism

There are a number of factors that cause employees to be absent from work:

Illness or injuries

Employees being absent is unavoidable due to illnesses or injuries.

Bullying or harassment

Management sometimes have to ask themselves if there is a specific reason for an employee being absent. The reason may be that the absent employee was bullied or harassed by a co-worker.

Disengagement

As soon as an employee is no longer committed to their job, they stop feeling responsible for the work and do not put in any effort. They do not feel any connection to the job and will look for excuses not to be at work. This disengagement can be due to disrespectful or unfair treatment, no feedback or lack of trust by management.

Case study

Low morale at eTV

May 2018

eTV has dropped its beleaguered breakfast show, Sunrise, and its staffers after a difficult ten years. The TV network has now outsourced and replaced the show with The Morning Show.

eTV's breakfast show change is part of ongoing restructuring, firings and resignations at eTV and its TV news channel eNCA. A senior and longtime eTV employee described the working environment at the broadcaster as "toxic, depressing, sad and not human".

Another eTV insider said that "morale is at an all-time low and people are desperately searching for new jobs".

Low employee morale

No employee wants to work in an environment that is tense, intimidating and/or has a low morale.

Child or elder care issues

Employees may be late for work or sometimes have to take time of work to take care of their children. The child might be sick or the daycare facility might be closed, which can cause parents to be absent. The same applies if the employee takes care of the elderly – a parent or a grandparent.

Stress

There are a number of reasons for stress and not all employees handle stress the same. Pressure at work, problems at home, job security, accidents, etc, are all examples of situations that may cause stress for the employee. Stress may affect employees in such a way that they more likely to be sick and absent from work.

Burnout

Some employees are workaholics and this behaviour tends to lead to burnout. Burnt-out employees are also more likely to become ill, because they are physically and mentally worn out.

Time theft

Some employees push the boundaries when it comes to being late for work, leaving early, or taking lengthy breaks.

Lack of flexibility

Employees who enjoy freedom or flexibility at work do not like it when they are forced in to fixed schedules or are not allowed to do things their way. Some will protest against this by being purposefully late or abusing breaks.

Methods of countering absenteeism and personnel turnover

Employee absenteeism and personnel turnover can cost an organisation time and money. The organisation has to be proactive and identify the causes behind absenteeism and personnel turnover. By being proactive they can be prepared and put tools in place to create a healthier workplace and ensure happier workers.

Appoint the right people

Start off by making sure the organisation appoints the correct person for the job. The human resources department has to make sure the candidate is well equipped with the correct qualifications, skills and experience for the position. The candidate also needs to be fully aware of what the job entails. Lastly, the candidate has to fit in with the organisation's culture.

> **DEFINITION**
>
> **morale –** a level of favourable (high morale) or unfavourable (low morale) attitudes and feelings

Be flexible with your employees

Management may allow employees to work from home if the position or type of work allows it. Flexibility appeals mostly to the younger generation workforce. Flexi-time reduces absenteeism as it allows employees to schedule their own working hours.

Teamwork

Create teams in your organisation that are appealing to be part of. They do not want to miss out on anything or let the team down, so they will not be absent without a good reason. They will work harder to impress the rest of the group. Employees who engage in non-work related social activities indicate that they enjoy each other's company.

Fulfill your workers' job expectations

One of the main reasons for an employee leaving the organisation is that the work they do is not what they were appointed for. The employee's job expectations are not met. They lose their interest and drive to perform.

Encourage work-life balance

Management has to encourage a balance in the employee's work and life outside the work. This is important for both the organsiation and the employee. Too much work will make employees feel burnt-out and tired, which means they are more likely to be sick and absent from work. An employee who gets time to rest, spend time with family and away from work, will be fresh, energised and rejuvenated.

Figure 4.9 Create a working environment that promotes a healthy work-life balance.

Prioritise your employees' health

It is important for the employee that the organisation prioritises their health and well-being. Providing them with health benefits will make them think twice before leaving the organisation.

Make opportunities for development and growth

An employee needs a challenging job where they can grow and where there are opportunities for them to climb the corporate ladder. It is important that the organisation invests time and effort into providing employees with these opportunities. If they do not, employees may not stay.

Clearly set attendance expectations

Create a clear attendance policy. It is important to communicate the organisation's expectations and requirements to the employees. Let the repercussions of absences be clear to them.

Enforce the attendance policy consistently

It is important for the organisation to have a policy that has flexibility built into it. This means the policy can be applied consistently and will not provoke claims of favouritism or discrimination when it is applied differently for different individuals. One manager might be more lenient towards absenteeism than another, which will lead to resentment if employees see this inconsistent behaviour.

Analyse absenteeism data

Patterns of absenteeism can only be made after all the data has been collected and accurately analysed.

Maintain a proper induction programme

A good and thorough induction process settles employees into the organisation. This will make them feel at home and cared for, which will reduce staff turnover and absenteeism.

Consider rewarding good attendance

It is important to penalise and discipline those employees who are absent without reason, but it is as important to reward those with good attendance practices. This can be a good motivator to encourage good attendance.

> **Key point:** Absenteeism and personnel turnover are costly, so employers need to be proactive in creating a healthy workplace to ensure that workers are happy.

UNIT 4.3 **Health and safety**

Occupational injuries and diseases might be the result of emotional and behavioural factors, but most can be traced to the physical work environment. Those characteristics of the work environment associated with injuries are known as **safety risks**. To avoid accidents, these risks must be removed. This can be achieved by, for example, placing protective screens on dangerous machinery, wearing protective clothing or promoting greater safety awareness among employees.

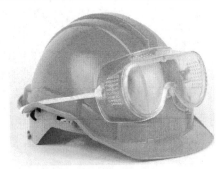

Figure 4.10 Protective clothing is important for workplace health and safety.

> **DEFINITION**
>
> **safety risks –** (also called health risks) those characteristics of the work environment that are associated with injuries and diseases among employees

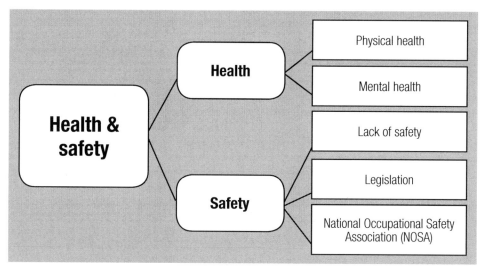

Figure 4.11 Health and safety characteristics

Health and safety issues have been in the news lately. See the two articles below that deal with alleged breaches of health and safety.

Noakes found not guilty of misconduct

21 April 2017

The HPCSA (Health Professions Council of South Africa) charged Professor Noakes with unprofessional conduct for giving 'unconventional advice' to a breastfeeding mother on a social media network (Twitter). Noakes tweeted in response to the breastfeeding mother and advised the mother to wean her baby onto a low carbohydrate, high fat diet.

Life Esidimeni: 144 patients dead

26 January 2018

144 mentally ill patients have died as a result of being moved from the Life Esidimeni hospital to various NGOs, the Health Ombudsman Professor Malegapuru Makgoba has found.

Multiple warnings about the dangers of cancelling the Life Esidimeni contract were raised before the patients were released from the institution. A formal inquiry has found that there were a number of breaches of protocol with moving the patients. The inquiry also found that families were excluded from decisions taken regarding the transfer. Psychiatrist Professor Christoffel Grobler testified that: "It doesn't take an expert to have known that there was some sort of risk involved at those facilities (NGOs)".

Because health and safety is such an important issue, the government has paid more attention to health and safety by promulgating legislation to determine standards and to establish measures for protecting the employee.

Who is responsible for health and safety in the work environment? In general, everyone in the organisation should be concerned with it. Formally, however, top management is responsible for instilling in employees an awareness of health and safety. Top management is also responsible for ensuring the organisation meets the health and safety requirements stipulated by government.

Figure 4.12 Everyone in an organisation is responsible for health and safety.

Health can be defined as the physical, mental and social well-being of the individual. Health has to do with the relationship between the body, mind and the social patterns of the human being. An employee's health can be affected by diseases, accidents and stress. It is important that management must not only see to the physical well-being of employees, but also to their psychological well-being.

Safety can be defined as the physical protection of employees against dangerous or potentially dangerous conditions and unsafe action of employees in the work environment, which may lead to accidents or injuries.

Unsafe working conditions include defective equipment, inadequate mechanical protection, explosions, fires, unsafe machinery and unsafe placement of machinery and equipment. Unsafe actions by employees include the wrong use of equipment and tools, as well as failure to comply with the safety regulations.

Guidelines for creating a healthy and safe work environment

The South African Institute of Safety Management says that the creation of healthy and safe work environments depends on the three E's: Engineering, Education and Enforcement.

Engineering: the equipment should be engineered for safety
Education: employees should be educated in safe procedures
Enforcement: safety rules should be enforced

Some general guidelines to creating a healthy and safe environment in the workplace are discussed below:

Reduce unsafe conditions.

Remove physical hazards that can cause accidents. Some organisations use a safety checklist to locate dangerous conditions.

Reduce unsafe acts through the correct selection and placement.

One way to reduce accidents is to screen out accident-prone persons before they are appointed. Accidents are similar to other types of poor performance. For example, emotional stability, muscular condition and visual skills are some of the skills to test before you hire a person for a particular dangerous job.

Train employees.

Experience reduces accidents. Training can provide a substitute for experience. Safety training can reduce accidents significantly.

Positive reinforcement.

Safety programmes where managers or supervisors praise employees for following the safety procedures or performing tasks safely have been used successfully to improve safety at work.

Commitment by top management.

Creating a healthy and safe work environment is largely the result of developing a safety-conscious attitude on the part of employees. This attitude will only materialise with the top management's full commitment.

Acting in accordance with health and safety laws.

Stipulated workplace standards and regulations are obligatory for all organisations. The guidelines range from ensuring hazards are identified (risk assessments) in the work environment, promoting proper hygiene, guaranteeing basic comfort levels to ensuring safe potable water and good ventilation.

Establish a clear health and safety policy.

This should apply to all employees – regardless of their level. If your policy changes, ensure everyone knows about it.

Stay fit.

Your employees may lead a desk-bound lifestyle, which could lead to long-term illness, especially if your environment is office-based. If the organisation can afford it, a fitness room or gym could be fitted into the office space to allow staff to become physically active.

Access to counselling services and/or specialist support groups.

These services and support groups can assist employees who suffer from alcoholism, drug addiction, HIV/AIDS or mental disorders.

Continually improve your health and safety system.

The health and safety system should be assessed annually and as needed. It is very important to investigate accidents, injuries, illnesses or any close encounters. Inspect daily or weekly if needed and make sure the equipment and processes are in order.

Medical facilities on site.

On-site medical facilities are there to monitor the health and safety of employees on an ongoing basis.

Power break 4.3   PAIR WORK

Read the information below. In pairs, answer the questions that follow.

Melinda Petersen has just been appointed as the health and safety manager at a new block of flats in Sea Point. The building is seven storeys high with an average of ten flats on each floor. Melinda's main objective is to make sure the building is as safe as possible for the tenants.

Which precautionary measures should Melinda take when the following situations occur?

1 When the floors are washed
2 When the lifts are serviced
3 When the building is fumigated

Elect health and safety representatives.

These representatives will regularly undertake safety inspections and are responsible for all health and safety measures being adhered to.

Factors that jeopardise health and safety

Some work environments, such as industries and mines, are more exposed to disease and accidents than others. Even work environments that are regarded as "healthy and safe", may result in unnecessary absences due to illness or accidents.

> **Did you know?** Employee action, or lack of action, accounts for 88% of workplace incidents. Only 10% of workplace incidents are the result of unsafe working conditions in South Africa.

Occupational health and safety may be jeopardised by factors such as:

Negative attitudes.

Employees with negative attitudes may be more prone to accidents or illness because they may tend to ignore health and safety regulations.

Poor training.

Poor training that does not keep up with technological advancements affects occupational health and safety because it may be the cause of accidents due to ignorance or inexperience.

Recklessness of employees.

Reckless employees contribute to higher incidences of health and safety breaches. An example of this could be construction workers who work without safety helmets and other protective clothing.

Unusual stress.

Stress due to factors such as abnormal work pressure, family problems, physical exhaustion or working conditions that may give rise to alcoholism or drug abuse, all contribute towards health and safety hazards.

Health, family and retirement benefits

Employees are the essence and key resource behind the organisation's ability to grow and prosper. So it is extremely important for the organisation to provide their employees with the necessary benefits. These benefits are also known as perks or fringe benefits and are provided to employees over and above their normal salaries and wages. Go back to Module 3, Unit 3.2 to read about fringe benefits again.

Most organisations provide different forms of fringe benefits or protection against loss of income or extra expenses due to illness or injuries sustained while on duty. The three most common forms of protection are:

Workmen's compensation

All organisations have to take into account the ever-changing external environment. The economy is developing and technology is evolving at a rapid pace. This requires an increase in production, which in turn increases the demand for labour. This is good for unemployment, but it also increases the risks related to occupational health and safety.

Any employer, casual or full-time worker, can claim from the Compensation for Injuries and Diseases Act (COIDA) if the injury or disease is considered to have happened in the course of employment. This fund offers five types of compensation: temporary disability, permanent disability, death, medical expenses and additional compensation.

Medical insurance

Medical insurance forms the base for any comprehensive benefits package for employees. The employee and their family's health is very important. Medical insurance provides them with the required peace of mind that they and their family will be taken care of when they are sick or injured.

Medical insurance will pay the required amounts of money to cover the medical expenses and/or treatments. Some organisation provides group health insurance policies, and offer employees many different options for insurance coverage. These policies differ in the way they cover their members, depending on medical plan and fund.

Did you know? There is a difference between medical insurance and medical schemes.

Medical cover is not always guaranteed with medical insurance. You might only be covered for certain procedures, and some people only discover on admission to a hospital that their medical costs are unlikely to be covered by the daily amount paid out by their hospital cash-back plans.

Medical schemes are regulated by the Medical Schemes Act of 1998. Medical schemes are not run for profit, and are required by the law to pay for the treatment of a list of 270 prescribed minimum benefits (PMBs), whether you have an expensive comprehensive plan, or a normal hospital plan. They also all have to pay for the treatment of 26 chronic conditions.

Retirement schemes

Most people look forward to the day they reach retirement. The big drawback is that from that point onwards, you are not able to earn any more money. A retirement scheme or pension is the income you will receive the day you are no longer working full time and earning a regular form of income. A retirement scheme makes provision for you to have a form of guaranteed payment. This depends on the retirement plan, but in many cases the scheme requires both the employer and employee to contribute money into a fund. Pension plans are considered a form of postponed income.

Substance abuse

Managers today deal with a complex set of problems. Among the most frustrating and difficult are the problems of worker alcoholism, drug addiction, and **substance abuse**. Most drugs and other chemical substances are helpful when used properly and for medical reasons, but when these substances are abused it can lead to serious issues, both for the employee and the organisation.

Substance abuse creates hazards for both the employee and the workplace. Substance abuse may lead to the impairment of both the co-ordination and the judgement of an employee. Employees who suffer with addiction make poor workers, because they are more subject to accidents, illness and absenteeism. They usually have a lot of excuses and develop an array of deceptions to hide their addictive problems. Figure 4.12 shows the signs managers must be aware of:

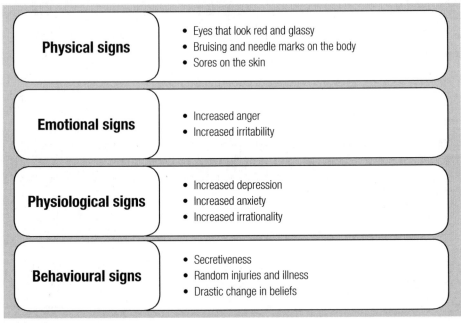

Physical signs	• Eyes that look red and glassy • Bruising and needle marks on the body • Sores on the skin
Emotional signs	• Increased anger • Increased irritability
Physiological signs	• Increased depression • Increased anxiety • Increased irrationality
Behavioural signs	• Secretiveness • Random injuries and illness • Drastic change in beliefs

Figure 4.13 Signs of substance abuse

Did you know? According to studies conducted by the International Labour Organisation (ILO) on the abuse of alcohol and drugs in the workplace, the following was found:
- Absenteeism of employees with alcohol and drug problems was three times higher than for other employees
- Employees with chemical dependence problems claimed sick benefits three times more than other employees and also made compensation claims five times more than other employees.

DEFINITION

substance abuse – the misuse of drugs such as alcohol and narcotics

Methods for prevention and treatment of substance abuse

As soon as you reduce employees' substance abuse, the costs for health care decrease, there will be less workplace injuries and overall productivity will improve. There are some practical solutions for preventing and addressing substance abuse:

- Confirm observations
  - Call upon another supervisor or manager, whenever possible, to witness and confirm observed deficiencies in employee performance and/or behaviour
  - Such observations should be documented
  - You should interview the employee in private to give the employee an opportunity to explain the observed behaviour.
- Inform the employee of the results of your assessment
  - Briefly explain that you and another manager/supervisor, if possible, have determined that the employee may be under the influence of alcohol or a controlled substance and is not able to perform their work in a safe and satisfactory manner.
- Implement a drug-free workplace and make sure there is a written substance abuse policy in place
  - This policy will emphasise that the use of alcohol or drugs is never permitted in the workplace
- Communicate information
  - Make sure all employees are aware of the health risks of alcohol and drug use
  - Use the organisation's websites and/or any health and wellness initiatives to communicate the information
- Educate employees about substance abuse
  - Educate them of the health and productivity dangers of drinking excessively and using illegal substances through company wellness programs
  - Also educate them about wellness strategies, such as learning about good nutrition, exercise, seat belt use, etc.
- Offer health benefits to employee that provide them with comprehensive coverage for substance use disorders, including aftercare and counselling
- Respect employees' privacy
  - It is important to protect an employee's privacy
  - Employers may not know who among their employees is in recovery from alcohol or drug abuse
  - If this information is known to management, they must acknowledge and appreciate the delicate balance between wanting to help and respecting an employee's need and desire for privacy.

The costs of substance abuse

Most people already know that substance abuse will destroy your health and can lead to serious mental health problems, such as depression and suicide, and it can ruin you financially too. It is no surprise then that substance abuse also has high costs in the workplace. Some of the effects of substance abuse are felt by the employee who is abusing substances themselves, but many are shared by the employer.

Figure 4.14 Substance abuse is detrimental to productivity in the workplace.

Some of the effects of substance abuse are:

- High employee turnover
- Higher rates of absenteeism
- Decrease in productivity and performance
- Increase in industrial fatalities and workplace accidents
- Higher workers' compensation costs
- Higher medical costs
- Increase in workplace theft and violence
- Greater legal liability
- Increased damage to equipment and machinery.

UNIT 4.4 **Career development**

A career can be defined as all the jobs that a person will hold in a lifetime plus the training and preparation necessary to qualify for such a job. Thus, a career path refers to the growth of the employee in an organisation. The path that a person takes in their career is the way we talk about the various different jobs and organisations that a person works for.

Career expectations encompass all things you want from a job such as responsibility, satisfaction, and good pay. Career planning is an individual's self-assessment and planning in terms of making a career choice, advancing in the career chosen or making a career change.

"They start on a career path so young these days."

Figure 4.15 Career development is an important part of each person's career path.

Career development is the formal approach by an organisation and involves the identification of career paths that employees can follow to achieve their career goals (e.g. to become the managing director of a large organisation such as Pick 'n Pay or Checkers). Career development can be seen as the proactive planning and implementation of the steps taken by the organisation towards the employee's career objectives.

Career management is the mindful planning of the employee's actions and decisions to accept certain jobs in the course of their life for better fulfilment, growth and financial stability. It is a process of events that start with the individual understanding themself, which includes job-related awareness.

Table 4.3 below outlines the differences between the career management and the development process.

Table 4.4 The differences between the career management process and the career development process

Career management process	Career development process
Employees:	Employers:
• Become aware of their own interests, values, strengths, and weaknesses • Identify career goals • Acquire information about job opportunities within the company • Establish action plans to achieve career goals.	• Use a formal approach to ensure that people with proper qualifications and experience are available when needed • Benefits both employees, as well as organisations • Need to have a career development programme and integrate the function with human resources activities

DEFINITIONS

career development – an organisation's approach to ensure qualified employees are available when needed

career management – the management of one's own career in order to reach career goals

The importance of career development

Helping your employees shape the future direction of their careers is a valuable activity. Unfortunately, it is an activity that is often ignored. As a result of this, organisations pay a high price – the loss of talented employees.

The purposes and objectives of career development can be listed as follows:
- To ensure talented employees are available for roles when needed
- To improve the ability of the organisation to recruit and retain high-talent employees
- To utilise human resources optimally
- To prepare employees for promotions
- To improve employee's self-confidence and motivation levels
- To improve (reduce) staff turnover
- To apply a balanced policy for promoting employees from within the organisation
- To make employees more flexible and adjustable to changes
- To better the employee's loyalty and commitment to the organisation
- To preserve harmonious industrial relations
- To introduce equitable employment practices that provide equal career opportunities for designated groups
- To help employees set more realistic career expectations.

The responsibilities of employees and managers with regard to career development

The responsibilities of managers
Managers play an important role in the following areas:

Setting the climate for the development of the employee
This is really about finding time for people. Developing people should be a priority for the organisation. When it is done properly, it can be a real pleasure!

Building a developmental relationship with employees
It is important to get to know your team. Encourage each individual to take responsibility for their own development, while providing assistance and creating suitable opportunities for them.

Giving feedback and focus
It is important that managers are open and honest about what standards and appropriate behaviour they expect of the employee. They'll frequently evaluate the employee's performance. Be honest when giving feedback and praise, but also handle poor performances firmly and quickly.

Delivering development
It is very important that the development priorities agreed on are actively pursued. Supervisors and managers should use every opportunity to pass on their own knowledge and experience and to educate employees informally.

Encouraging active career development

Expose individuals in the current job to a wider career context – ask the questions: what has this individual done before, and what might they do in the future? Managers and supervisors should put individuals in touch with others, at more senior levels or in other parts of the business, who can help them develop their careers.

Make finances available

Managers are to see that the necessary funds are available to enable instructors to develop programmes and to purchase sophisticated learning and development aids.

The responsibilities of employees

It is the employee's personal responsibility to respond to and take advantage of the opportunities offered by management by:

Taking initiative

Employees have the responsibility to speak up to management about their goals and desire to progress in their career. Management should take note of them because of their excellent individual and/or team performances.

Having a positive attitude

It is crucial for an individual to be positive when they approach their development. A negative or wrong attitude can seriously hamper an employee's professional growth. For example, if an employer gives an employee additional responsibilities, it is up to them to see it as an opportunity to learn and grow rather than being forced to do extra work.

Outside learning

Employees should not expect only their employer to develop them. It is the employee's responsibility to use their own personal time to learn. For example, an employer can offer to pay for the employee's college tuition, but the employee is the one that should put in their own hours studying and working toward their certificate, diploma or degree.

Not getting involved in workplace politics

Employers cannot develop and invest in all the employees at once, plus not all employees are interested in growing personally and professionally. When another employee is part of a development programme and you are not, it might make you feel left out. Employees have a responsibility not to be part of gossip and/or treating others who take advantage of development programmes.

Career development methods

A key method in career development is training. Training is the action of teaching a person a particular skill or type of behaviour.

In South Africa there are three categories of training and development, as shown in Figure 4.14.

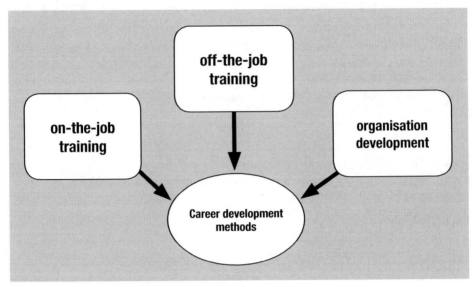

Figure 4.16 Three categories of training and development

On-the-job training

On-the-job training is usually directly related to the job. The trainees receive training in their work environment. Trainees learn by doing. They learn continuously and over a long period of time. On-the-job training requires no special equipment. Trainees are extensively influenced by their immediate superior. The superior is directly responsible for the training of their subordinates. On-the-job training however, prevents trainees from obtaining a broad perspective and can poorly influence their perception of their job and how it fits in the organisation.

The following methods are generally used for on-the-job training:

- Coaching
- Job rotation
- Junior boards
- Job instruction training
- Understudy
- Learner-controlled instruction
- Apprenticeship training
- Internships.

Off-the-job training

Off-the-job training is usually done in a classroom situation. It can be on the premises of the organisation but away from the learner's place of work, or it can be totally removed from the organisation, such as a conference centre. These methods can also be seen as classroom or simulation methods, since they simulate real-life situations. Off-the-job training may be used to develop the ability, interpersonal skills and attitudes of the trainee.

The following methods are generally used for off-the-job training:

- Case studies
- The incident method
- Role play
- In-basket training
- Management games
- Conference methods
- Brainstorming
- Assessment centres
- Lectures.

Off-the-job training differs from on-the-job training in a number of ways, as detailed in Table 4.5 below:

Table 4.5 The differences between on-the-job training and off-the-job training

On-the-job training method:	Off-the-job training method:
Learning by doing	Learning by acquiring knowledge
Practical	Theory
Carried out by experienced employees	Carried out by professionals/experts
Cost: Inexpensive	Cost: Expensive
Manufacturing firms	Non-manufacturing firms
No work disruption—trainees produce the products during learning	Work disruption—first training is provided, which is followed by a performance
Takes place at workstation	Takes place in classroom
Requires special equipment	Requires no special equipment
Immediate feedback	Little feedback
Time: Long period (continuously)	Time: Short period

Organisation development (OD)

Organisation development (OD) is the process that prepares organisations to take on and accept change. It is a planned process of using knowledge and technology of applied behavioural science to improve the organisational effectiveness and health through changes in individual and group behaviour, culture, and systems of the organisation.

Organisation development is aimed at open communication between the different levels in the organisation structure and to improve the ability of employees to adapt to change. OD is therefore used to guide employees in the development of their careers.

The following methods are generally used for organisation development:

- Survey feedback
- Behavioural modelling
- Sensitivity training
- Grid training
- Team building
- Laboratory training
- Managerial grid.

The main objectives of organisation development

The main aims of organisation development are:

- To improve trust among the members of an organisation at an interpersonal level
- To increase all members' level of commitment and satisfaction
- To promote members to confront and fix problems instead of postponing and neglecting them
- To handle conflict in an effective way
- To increase the teamwork and co-operation among employees within the working environment
- To promote a problem-solving culture within the organisation
- To improve awareness of the organisation's vision among its members. OD aims to align the employees' vision with that of the organisation's
- To make the transition from formal authority to personal skills and knowledge more effortlessly
- To achieve a trustworthy working environment that allows new operations.

Figure 4.17 Career development is important for the growth and success of an organisation.

Practical enhancement of career development

The steps below identify a practical strategy that management can use and follow in order to ensure effective career management in their organisation.

Step 1:	Identify the goals of individual employees and match them with the goals of the organisation.
Step 2:	Link career development with management and the human resource management department section.
Step 3:	Link career development with future trends and present values.
Step 4:	Provide effective communication between employees and managers.
Step 5:	Commitment of employers to career development.

WHAT DO WE KNOW AND WHERE TO NEXT...

Revisiting the learning objectives

Now that you have completed this module you should have achieved the learning objectives listed in the table below:

Learning objective	What you have learned	Tick box
Explain the impact of job satisfaction and its relationship to worker productivity/ effectiveness and commitment.	Job satisfaction: • Describes the employee's contentment/satisfaction with their job or with particular aspects of the job • Creates a hard worker who gets good results and therefore productivity is increased • One of the factors that enables employees to perform at the highest level • Helps workers to be productive and committed to their work.	☐
Explain how job satisfaction of employees can be measured or assessed by management.	Job satisfaction can be measured: • Formally, such as in an employee survey • Informally, in a weekly or monthly staff meeting.	☐
Explain major causes of job satisfaction in practice.	Factors influencing job satisfaction: • Monetary benefits • Fair treatment • The feeling of belonging • Adequate working conditions • Initiation and leadership • Stability • Safety and security • Challenges • Responsibilities • Creativity.	☐
Indicate the relevance of job enrichment to job satisfaction.	Job enrichment is the purposeful restructuring of an employee's job to make it more challenging, meaningful and interesting. Job enrichment is important for increasing job satisfaction, but for an employee to react well to job enrichment the following conditions must be in place: • The specific employee must want to be part of job enrichment • The employee should be consulted before implementation so that he/she can propose suggestions • Employees must understand the job in its entirety • The job must be meaningful so that the employee feels they are performing an important task	☐

Learning objective	What you have learned	Tick box
	• Employees must have independence and freedom so that they can make their own decisions in the job • The job must offer variety, which means that a number of different skills will be used • Management has to offer chances and opportunities for employees to grow and develop • There must be feedback on the job they are doing.	
Review the influence of job rotation as a method of training for job satisfaction.	**Job rotation** means employees are transferred from job to job on a systematic basis. The advantages of job rotation: • Job rotation gives some variation to the job • It exposes the employee to a wider experience • Job rotation helps management to see the employee's skills and abilities • Management has the opportunity to determine the talent of employees • Management has more certainty where to utilise the employee • Job rotation turns specialists into generalists • The employee can perform a variety of tasks • Job rotation builds the employee's self-belief • Employees will be more motivated • Employees will also be more flexible. The disadvantages of job rotation: • Employees are only moving from job to job at the same level, which means it is the same type of job • The regular moving from job to job causes interruptions • Employees have a tendency to take up a lot of time to get familiar with the new job • Management wastes a lot of time in convincing and motivating employees for job rotation • Job rotation increases costs and decreases productivity • Just as an employee becomes effective and efficient at their station/job, they have to rotate to a new one • The constant change can cause stress and anxiety • An employee who is interested in a particular job but who has to go through the rotation process might become demotivated.	☐ ☐ ☐
Demonstrate how to measure absenteeism and labour turnover and the cost thereof in practice.	• Personnel turnover refers to the number or percentage of workers who leave an organisation and are replaced by new employees. • Absenteeism is the failure of employees to report work, or staying away from work, without good reason or permission.	☐ ☐

Learning objective	What you have learned	Tick box
	Formula for calculating turnover and absenteeism:	☐
	Turnover: Calculate the number of staff that left the company as a percentage of the total number of staff.	
	Number of staff who left divided by total staff. Multiply this by 100/1 to get a percentage.	☐
	Absenteeism: Calculate the number of hours or days as a percentage of the total hours or days worked.	
	Total hours/days employees are absent divided by total hours/days worked. Multiply that by 100/1 to get a percentage.	
Describe the factors which exert an influence on employee absenteeism and labour turnover in practice.	Factors causing personnel turnover: • Dissatisfaction with wages • Dissatisfaction with working environment • Dissatisfaction with the job • Dissatisfaction with personnel policies • Lack of medical, recreational and other facilities • Lack of transport services • Dissatisfaction with working hours.	☐
	Factors causing absenteeism: • Illness or injuries • Bullying or harassment • Disengagement • Low employee morale • Child or elder care issues • Stress • Burnout • Time theft • Lack of flexibility.	☐
Describe methods of countering personnel turnover and absenteeism.	Methods of countering personnel turnover and absenteeism: • Appoint the right people • Be flexible with your employees • Implement flexi-time • Teamwork • Fulfil your workers' job expectations • Encourage work-life balance • Prioritise your employees' health • Make opportunities for development and growth • Clearly set attendance expectations • Enforce the attendance policy consistently • Analyse absenteeism data • Maintain a proper induction programme • Consider rewarding good attendance.	☐

Learning objective	What you have learned	Tick box
Recognise the importance of employee health with regard to employee effectiveness in practice.	Effective practices for employee health: • Reduce unsafe conditions • Reduce unsafe acts through the correct selection and placement • Train employees • Positive reinforcement • Commitment by top management • Act in accordance with health and safety laws • Establish a clear health and safety policy • Stay fit • Access to counselling services and/or specialist support groups • Continually improve your health and safety system • Medical facilities on site • Elect health and safety representatives.	☐ ☐
Explain the importance of health and family care benefits and retirement benefits as part of a remuneration package (see incentive schemes).	Three common forms of benefits: Workmen's compensation: • Any employer; casual and full-time worker, can claim from the Compensation for Injuries and Diseases Act (COIDA) if the injury or disease is considered to have happened in the course of employment. This fund offers five types of compensation: temporary disability, permanent disability, death, medical expenses and additional compensation. Medical insurance: • Medical insurance is an insurance policy that will pay specified amounts of money to cover medical expenses or treatments. Retirement schemes: • A retirement scheme or pension is the income you will receive the day you no longer working full time and earning a regular form of income. A retirement scheme make provision for you to have a form of guaranteed payment.	☐ ☐ ☐
Briefly discuss the implications of substance abuse in the workplace.	The costs of substance abuse: • High employee turnover • Higher rates of absenteeism • Decrease in productivity and performance • Increase in industrial fatalities and workplace accidents • Higher workers' compensation costs • Higher medical costs • Increase in workplace theft and violence • Greater legal liability • Increased damage to equipment and machinery.	☐
Briefly describe the meaning of career development in the work environment.	**Career development** can be seen as the proactive planning and action steps towards your career objectives. Managers are responsible for: • Setting the climate for the development of the employee • Building a developmental relationship with employees • Giving feedback and focus • Delivering development • Encouraging active career development • Make finances available.	☐ ☐

Learning objective	What you have learned	Tick box
	Employees are responsible for: • Taking initiative • Having a positive attitude • Outside learning • Not getting involve in workplace politics • Accepting the final responsibility for their career planning and development.	☐
	On-the-job training method: • Learning by doing • Practical • Carried out by experienced employees • Manufacturing firms • No work disruption—trainees produce the products during learning • Takes place at workstation • Require special equipment • Immediate feedback • Cost: Inexpensive • Time: Long period (continuous).	☐
	Off-the-job training method: • Learning by acquiring knowledge • Theory • Carried out by professionals/experts • Non-manufacturing firms • Work disruption—first training is provided, which is followed by a performance • Takes place in classroom • Requires no special equipment • Little feedback • Cost: Expensive • Time: Short period.	☐
Discuss in a pragmatic way the importance of career development to both employers and employees.	Step 1: Identify the goals of individual employees and match them with the goals of the organisation Step 2: Link career development with management and the human resource management department section Step 3: Link career development with future trends and present values Step 4: Provide effective communication between employees and managers Step 5: Commitment of employers to career development.	☐

Assessment

True or false questions

Choose whether the following statements are TRUE or FALSE. Write only the question number and 'true' or 'false'.

1. Accidents are three times more likely to occur in a workplace where there is substance abuse.
2. Absenteeism is due to substance abuse, lack of communication and personnel problems.
3. Organisation development is a planned effort to increase effectiveness through planned interventions.
4. Job satisfaction reduces absenteeism but has no effect on labour turnover.
5. Quality of work life refers to the positive or negative feelings employees have about their workplace.

(5 × 2) [10]

Multiple choice questions

Choose the correct answer from the options provided. Choose only A, B, C or D and write your answer next to the question number:

1. Employees must have independence and freedom so that they can make their own decisions in the job.
   A   Job rotation
   B   Job enrichment
   C   Job satisfaction
   D   Job specification   (2)
2. The proactive planning and implementation of action steps towards your career goals.
   A   Career
   B   Career path
   C   Career management
   D   Career development   (2)
3. A lifetime plus the training and preparation necessary to qualify for such a job.
   A   Career
   B   Career path
   C   Career management
   D   Career development   (2)
4. The things you want from a job, such as responsibility, satisfaction, and good pay.
   A   Career
   B   Career path
   C   Career management
   D   Career expectations   (2)

5. Another word for your working life, the various jobs you take and your
    vocational choices.
    A   Career
    B   Career path
    C   Career management
    D   Career expectations   (2)
                                                              (5 × 2) [10]

Short questions

Briefly answer the following questions:
1. Name five actions that may jeopardise health and safety in the workplace.   (5)
2. Briefly discuss job satisfaction.   (4)
3. Distinguish between career development and career management.   (2 × 2)
4. Name seven factors that cause absenteeism.   (7)
                                                                         [20]

Long questions

Answer the following questions as comprehensively as you can:
1. State TEN methods an organisation can apply to overcome absenteeism.   (10)
2. Provide EIGHT negative outcomes of substance abuse.   (8 × 2)
3. State the responsibilities of employees with regard to career development.   (6 × 2)
4. What are the differences between on-the-job and off-the-job training?
    Answer in the form of a table.   (5 × 2 × 2)
5. State SIX disadvantages of job rotation.   (6 × 2)
                                                                         [70]
                                                      Grand total: 110 marks

REFERENCES

Abdullah, W. and Mohamed, F. 2002. *Human Resources Management: A Comprehensive Guide*. Heinemann Publishers.

Accounting Management: http://accountlearning.blogspot.co.za/2013/01/factors-affecting-recruitment.html (Accessed 1 June 2018).

Andrews, Y. 1997. *Personnel Management in South Africa: A Study Guide for College Students*. Bethlehem: Curmo Designs.

Dessler, G. 1988. *Personnel Management*. 4th ed. Cornell University: Prentice-Hall International Editions.

Dworzanowski-Venter, B. 2015. *Succeed in Labour Relations N5*. Cape Town: Oxford University Press.

Erasmus B.J. and Schenk, H.W. 2008. *South African Human Resource Management: Theory and Practice*. Cape Town: Juta and Company, Ltd.

Flippo, E.B. 1980. *Personnel Management*. 6th ed. University of Virginia: McGraw-Hill series in management.

Gerber, P.D., Nel, P.S. and van Wyk, P.S. 2014. *Human Resources Management*. 3rd ed. Southern Book Publishers (Pty) Ltd.

Groover, M.P. 2007. *Work Systems and the Methods, Measurement, and Management of Work*. Pearson Prentice Hall.

HR Learner's Guide. https://hrlearnersguide.wordpress.com/2012/08/18/factors-affecting-recruitment/ (Accessed 1 June 2018).

HR Tech Outlook. https://employee-engagement.hrtechoutlook.com/cxoinsights/the-growing-impact-of-technology-on-recruitment-nid-121.html (Accessed 1 June 2018).

Kroon, J. (ed). 1990. *General Management*. 2nd ed. Cape Town: Kagiso Tertiary.

Merriam-Webster Dictionaries. https://www.merriam-webster.com/ (Accessed 1 June 2018).

Mornell, P. 1998. *Hiring Smart!: How to Predict Winners and Losers in the Incredibly Expensive People-Reading Game*. Berkeley: Ten Speeds Press.

Occupational Health and Safety: Workplace Health https://www.ocsa.co.za (Accessed 1 June 2018).

Office Vibe. 12 Recruiting Statistics That Will Change The Way You Hire. https://www.officevibe.com/blog/12-recruiting-stats (Accessed 1 June 2018).

Sources of Recruitment of Employees: Internal and External Sources. http://www.yourarticlelibrary.com/recruitment/sources-of-recruitment-of-employees-internal-and-external-sources-recruitment/25954/ (Accessed 1 June 2018).

South African Department of Labour Online. Basic Guide to Affirmative Action. http://www.labour.gov.za/DOL/legislation/acts/basic-guides/basic-guide-to-affirmative-action (Accessed 1 June 2018).

Undercover Recruiter. 5 Global Stats Shaping Recruiting Trends. http://theundercoverrecruiter.com/global-stats-recruiting-trends/ (Accessed 1 June 2018).

Wikipedia. Applicant tracking system. https://en.wikipedia.org/wiki/Applicant_tracking_system
Trade unions in South Africa. https://en.wikipedia.org/wiki/Trade_unions_in_South_Africa (Accessed 1 June 2018).

ACKNOWLEDGMENTS

Images: page 2: Shutterstock 692982994 / Dragon Images; page 5: logo of Statistics SA; page 8: Shutterstock 505117981 / ShutterStockStudio; page 11: Pixabay / RawPixel, Shutterstock 480090436 / Rawpixel; page 13: Shutterstock 383394934 / michaeljung; page 16: Pixabay / StartupStockPhotos; page 18: Pixabay / Maylai; page 20: Pixabay / Maklay62; page 22: Shutterstock 231569581 / Hywards, Shutterstock 363719150 / Rohappy; page 24: Shutterstock / Mclek, Shutterstock 179368157 / Alfonso de Tomas; page 35: Shutterstock 692983150 / Dragon Images; page 41: Shutterstock 58185892 / Anglian Art; page 42: Pixabay / GDJ; page 45: Shutterstock 152549060 / Artfamily; page 51: Shutterstock 636072635 / Impact photography; page 52: Pixabay / TryJimmy; page 58: Pixabay / Clker-Free-Vector-Images-3736; page 59: Shutterstock 61968841 / StockLite; page 61: Shutterstock 56038 / Zurijeta; page 64: Shutterstock / Andrey_Popov; page 68: Shutterstock 117536314 / Stuart Jenner; page 80: Shutterstock 692983099 / Dragon Images; page 85: Shutterstock 56114470 / Joachim Wendler; page 98: Shutterstock / By Bakhtiar Zein; page 108: Shutterstock 14718100 / Nikoner; page 109: Pixabay / stevepb; page 122: Pixabay / ranjatm, Shutterstock 221458231 / michaeljung; page 125: Shutterstock 703938226 / Dim Tik; page 127: Shutterstock 572387341 / Yuttana Contributor studio; page 131: Medical boarding; page 141: Shutterstock 181457837 / Monkey Business Images; page 144: Shutterstock 287274665 / Pressmaster; page 145: Shutterstock 63081709 / Chiakto, Shutterstock 174539258 / Monkey Business Images; page 146: Shutterstock 332552936 / Johan Swanepoel; page 149: Shutterstock 54771 / iQoncept; page 154: Shutterstock 529417576 / Visual Generation; page 155: Shutterstock 287213735 / Ronnachai Palas; page 159: Shutterstock 173798813 / docstockmedia; page 160: Shutterstock 200373776 / kungverylucky; page 162: Pixabay / TheDigitalArtist; page 168: Pixabay / Stevepb; page 174: Shutterstock 106965104 / rnl

GLOSSARY

absentee rate the percentage of the organisation's total staff that is absent for a particular period of time

absenteeism the failure of employees to report to work without good reason or permission

achievement to accomplish something

affirmative action the labour policy aimed at redressing the inequalities of the past and, in so doing, achieving a transformed workplace, which is representative of the greater South Africa

average the sum of the numbers divided by how many numbers are being considered

bonus a sum of money over and above an employee's normal salary as a reward for good performance

career development an organisation's approach to ensure qualified employees are available when needed

career management the management of one's own career in order to reach career goals

commission a fee, normally a set percentage of the value involved, paid to a broker or agent for their service in facilitating a transaction

compensable factors factors (things) that you may receive compensation (payment) for

compensation package the total compensation that an employer offers to an employee, including bonuses, commission, salary and benefits

demotion the movement of an employee to a lower position in the organisation's structure with less responsibility, authority and a decrease in salary and status

discrimination the unfair treatment of a person (or a group of people) based on their skin colour, sex, religion, etc.

dismissal the involuntary termination of service, also known as firing

electronic media ways of sharing information that are not in print, such as radio, television, and the internet

employee compensation all forms of remuneration or reward that an employee might receive for work done, for example, salaries and wages

employment the hiring of an individual to provide an organisation with their time, skills and services in exchange for compensation

feedback the response to something, such as a product, process or an employee's performance to evaluate if it was successful or not

financial rewards money that is given to employees

formative evaluation the assessment in the development stage of someone's learning

fringe benefits a fringe benefit is a non-monetary form of compensation in addition to your salary, such as company car, house allowance and medical insurance

gross pay the amount of money the employee receives before any taxes and deductions are made

incentive an incentive is a type of reward or payment to an employee to motivate or encourage someone to do something or to stimulate greater performances

incentive scheme a programme to encourage and motivate employees to work at their maximum capacity and to be as productive as possible

induction the process of welcoming and receiving the new employee to the organisation and preparing them for their new role

job enlargement added duties and responsibilities that are not in your current job description

job enrichment the purposeful restructuring of an employee's job to make it more challenging, meaningful and interesting

job rotation employees are transferred from job to job on a systematic basis

job satisfaction the employee's contentment/ satisfaction with their job or with particular aspects of the job

management by objectives (MBO) a personnel management technique where managers and employees decide together the goals for a specific period of time, e.g. a year or quarter

median the middle number of a list of numbers

morale a level of favourable (high morale) or unfavourable (low morale) attitudes and feelings

nett pay (take-home pay) the amount of money the employee receives after all deductions, such as income tax and unemployment insurance (UIF)

non-financial rewards the benefits given to the employees of the organisation to increase the employee job performance, employee loyalty towards the organisation, employee morale, etc. Not money given directly to the employees.

notice period the time period the employee gives the employer when they resign. This is time between the resigning and the last working day.

percentage a mathematical term used to express a number as a fraction out of one hundred

performance appraisal a formal process used by the organisation to identify, measure and record an employee's job-related strengths and weaknesses

performance management (reward management) an organisation's strategies and policies to reward employees in a fair and equal manner

personnel research the systematic gathering of information and facts to find a solution to a personnel problem

personnel turnover (also called staff turnover, labour turnover) the number or percentage of workers who leave an organisation and are replaced by new employees

placement the process of assigning a specific job to a selected candidate

policy the broad guidelines of an organisation

print media text and images printed on paper, such as newspaper, magazines, printed journals and pamphlets

productivity level of achievement, results or creativity

promotion the most common form of internal recruitment where an employee is moved to an upper level of the organisation with more responsibility and prestige

ratio the relationship between two numbers. A ratio indicates how many times one number contains another number.

recruitment the cost effective search for people who have the necessary potential, knowledge, skills and abilities to fill positions as employees within an organisation

regressions the statistical tools used to estimate the strength and the direction of the relationship between two linearly-related variables

reliability the degree to which the assessment tool produces stable and consistent results

resignation when an employee decides that they will not continue working at the company or organisation

retirement when an employee stops working, usually because the person reaches a certain age

reward management an organisation's strategies and policies to reward the employees in a fair and equal manner

safety risks (also called health risks) this refers to those characteristics of the work environment that are associated with injuries and diseases among employees

salary a fixed amount paid at regular intervals, typically on a monthly basis

screening the part of the recruitment process where candidates who do not meet the minimum requirements for the position are eliminated

selection the process of putting the right candidate in the right position. It is a procedure of matching organisational requirements with the skills and qualifications of the potential candidate

staff turnover employee turnover refers to the number/percentage of employees who leave an organisation and are replaced by new employees

statistical analysis a process of collecting, examining, manipulating and interpreting data with the goal of discovering useful information. Statistical analysis changes raw data into meaningful information.

substance abuse the misuse of drugs such as alcohol or narcotics

termination of service any kind of separation between the employee and the employer

transfer the horizontal movement of an employee between departments or branches

trends the general direction in a series of data points on a graph

validity the extent to which the assessment tool accurately measures what it is supposed to measure

viable possible or likely to succeed

INDEX